HEINEMANN COUNTRY STUDIES

CHINA

Trevor Higginbottom
Tony White
Series Editor: John Hopkin

Heinemann Educational Publishers
Halley Court, Jordan Hill, Oxford, OX2 8EJ
A division of Reed Educational & Professional Publishing Ltd
Heinemann is a registered trademark of Reed Educational & Professional Publishing Ltd

OXFORD MELBOURNE AUCKLAND
JOHANNESBURG BLANTYRE GABORONE
IBADAN PORTSMOUTH NH (USA)
CHICAGO

First published 1999

ISBN 0 435 35624 0

03 02 01 00 99
10 9 8 7 6 5 4 3 2 1

Typeset and illustrated by Hardlines, Charlbury, Oxford OX7 3PS

Printed and bound in Spain by Edelvives

Acknowledgements
The authors wish to thank Associate Professor George Lin, University of Hong Kong, for his advice and support in writing this book.

The publishers would like to thank the following for permission to reproduce copyright material.

Maps and extracts

p.4 John Bryan Starr, Understanding China / Profile Books, London 1997, 1999; **p.6 C** Fang Jun Yi, An Outline of China's Geography / Era Book Company Limited, Hong Kong, 1980; **p.11 D** Mike Senior, Trends in Geography 2 / Pearson Education, Hong Kong; **p.16 A** Robert Prosser, Places and Cases: The World / Stanley Thornes Publishers Limited, Cheltenham; **p.17 B** Professional Geographer 48(1) / Blackwell Publishers, Boston, USA, 1996; **p.17 A** South China Morning Post; **p.18** South China Morning Post; **p.20** Butterworth Heinemann Asia; **p.27 A** Associated Press, New York; **p.32** South China Morning Post; **p.33** South China Morning Post; **p.35 C** Brookes, Clammer, Currie, Higginbottom et al, Geography Today / Collins Educational, London; **p.44** China Today / The China Welfare Institute, Beijing, 1999; **p.50** Paul Theroux, Going to See the Dragon / Harper's Magazine, 1993, New York; **p.56 A** South China Morning Post; **p.56 B** South China Morning Post; **p.57 C** Sunday Standard, Hong Kong, 1993; **p.58 B** © The Economist, London (1 May 1999); **p.59 C** South China Morning Post.

Photographs
Cover photos: Shanghai street scene: Tony Stone Images; Chinese girl: The Image Bank.
p. 4 B Getty Images; **p. 6 A** APL; **p. 6 B** Getty Images; **p. 6 D** China Photo Library; **p. 7 E** Tony Stone; **p. 9 C** APL; **p. 10 A** South China Morning Post Picture Library; **p. 10 B** South China Morning Post Picture Library; **p. 13 C** Getty Images; **p. 14** Chinese Government; **p. 15 B** South China Morning Post Picture Library; **p. 17 D** South China Morning Post Picture Library; **p. 19 C** Hong Kong survey and mapping office; **p. 19 D** Hong Kong survey and mapping office; **p. 20 A** Getty Images; **p. 22 A** Hong Kong Survey and mapping office; **p. 23 D** Getty Images; **p. 24 A** Eye Ubiquitous; **p. 26 A** South China Morning Post Picture Library; **p. 29 D** Eye Ubiquitous; **p. 30 C** South China Morning Post Picture Library; **p. 32 A** Getty Images; **p. 39 E** South China Morning Post Picture Library; **p. 40 D** Getty Images; **p. 41 E** China Photo Library; **p. 43 D(i)** Getty Images; **p. 43 D(ii)** Getty Images; **p. 43 D(iii)** China Photo Library; **p. 45 A** Stock House Ltd; **p. 46 B** Trevor Higginbottom; **p. 48 A** APL; **p. 48 B** South China Morning Post Picture Library; **p. 50 C** China Photo Library **p. 52 A** APL; **p. 56 D(i)** Xinhua Picture Agency, **(ii)** Agence France-Presse **p. 59 E** South China Morning Post Picture Library

The publishers have made every effort to trace the copyright holders. However if any material has been overlooked or incorrectly acknowledged, we would be pleased to correct this at the earliest opportunity.

Tel: 01865 888058 email: info.he@heinemann.co.uk

Contents

1 INTRODUCING CHINA

An emerging giant

▶ Why is China such an important country for us to study?

China is home to almost a quarter of the world's population. Within the next few decades the country could become a global economic and political **superpower**. The growth of China will, almost certainly, have a great impact on the world in the early part of the twenty-first century.

In the last ten years there has been a great deal of investment in China by foreign countries and firms. The country itself is investing abroad. This had led to changing lifestyles for individuals.

A China in the world, 1996

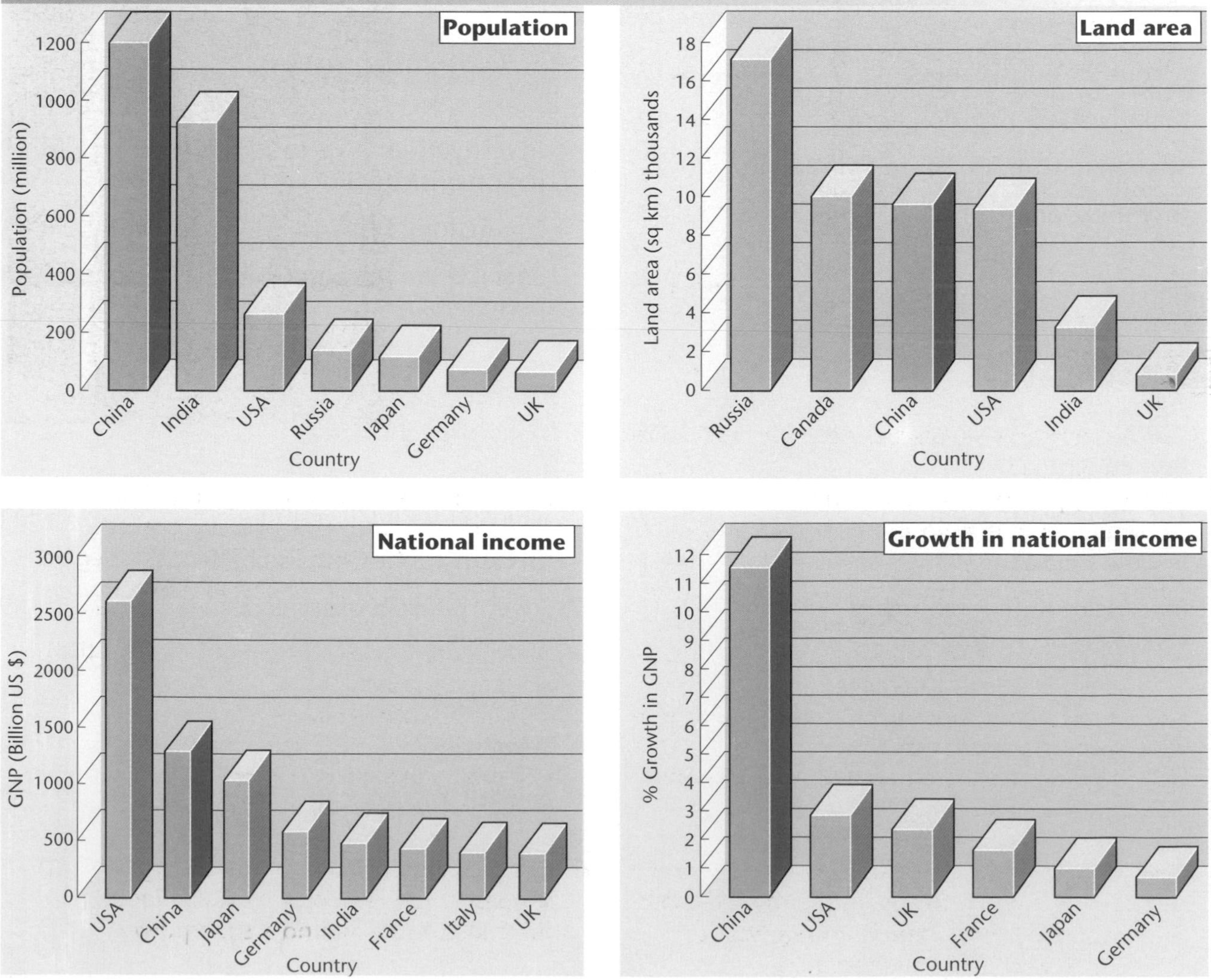

"There has been a great deal of good news coming out of China in recent years:

- China has one of the world's fastest growing economies. Indeed, there are those who predict that, at its current rate of growth, China's will be the world's largest economy by 2040, surpassing those of Japan and of the United States.
- Economic growth has greatly improved the standard of living for most, if not all, Chinese people. Rural incomes are three times what they were in 1978, the beginning of the current period of economic reform, and urban incomes are up nearly five times.
- There has also been some relaxation of the tight control the Chinese government maintained over its population. Most of the Chinese people are enjoying much more freedom from government interference in their lives than they did fifteen years ago."

Understanding China, John Bryan Starr, 1998

B Administrative regions and main cities of China

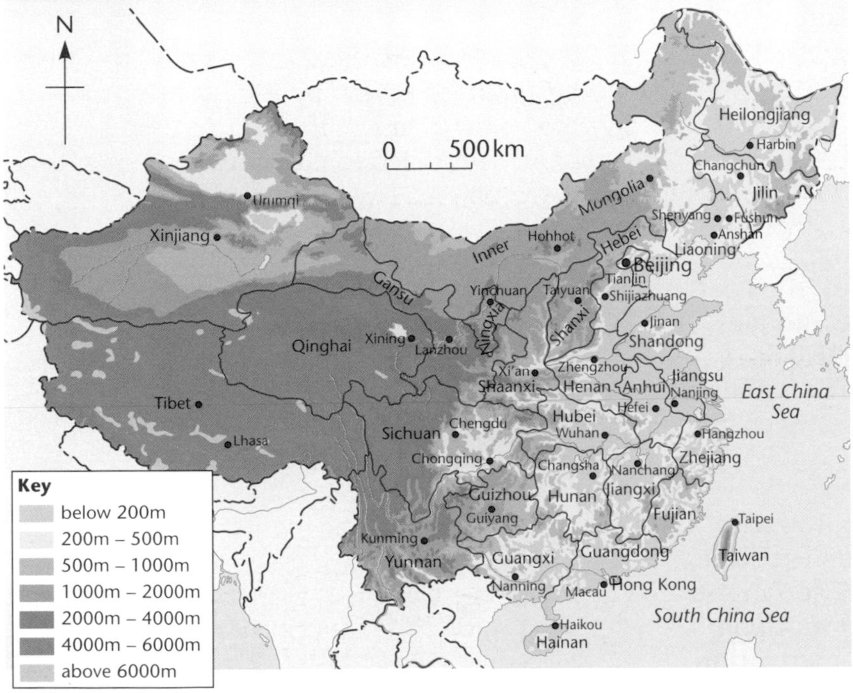

C McDonald's in Beijing

ACTIVITIES

1 As a class exercise, discuss how you see China as a country.

a) On your own, write down five words that come into your mind when you think of 'China'.

b) In groups, compare your responses. Write one list of your words that gave a positive impression of the country and a second list which gave a negative impression.

c) Discuss how you might have formed these impressions of China.

d) Consider how accurate your impressions of the country might be.

2 a) Work in pairs. Using the information on these pages, write down the main reasons why you think China is an important country to study in geography.

b) Explain what is meant by 'a global economic and political superpower'.

c) Explain why firms like McDonald's regard China as such an important country.

3 Write sentences to compare China and the United Kingdom's:
- total population in 1996;
- land area;
- national income in 1996;
- growth in national income in 1996.

4 Using the information on these pages, suggest three reasons why China faces difficulties in becoming a superpower.

China's physical landscapes

- What are the main physical regions of China?
- What types of landscapes do they contain?

China can be divided into a number of physical regions, each with a distinctive landscape. Two thirds of the country's total area consists of mountains and **plateaux**. The remaining third is an area of river basins and plains.

As shown in cross-section **C**, the physical geography of China can be thought of as a series of three steps. The first step is the Plateau of Tibet, with an average height of 4000 metres. The second step includes the Mongolian Plateau, the Tarim Basin, the Loess Plateau, the Sichuan Basin and the Yunnan-Guizhou Plateau, all of which descend to heights of 900 metres. The third step is mainly an area of **river plains** at heights between 700 and 800 metres.

China's two longest rivers flow from west to east across these three steps, at different stages in gorges, basins and floodplains. The Yangtze River, 6380km in length, is a main transport route and a rich source of water for **irrigation** and hydro-electric power. The Yellow River, 5465km in length, gets its name from the load of sediment it picks up as it crosses the **Loess** Plateau, which is covered by great thicknesses of wind-borne dust blown from central Asia (see pages 28 and 29).

B The Tibetan Plateau

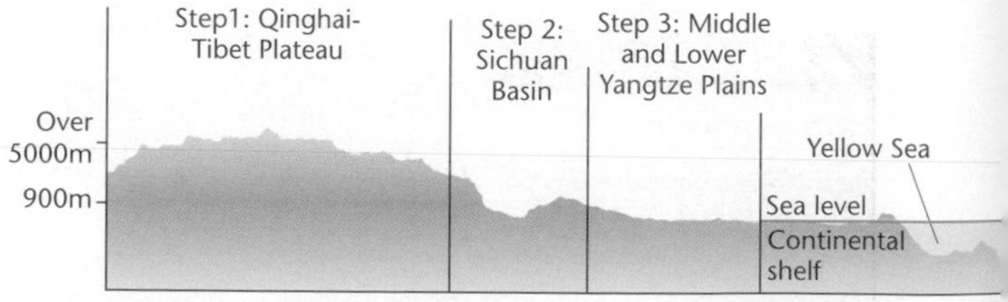

C A cross-section of China at 30°N

A The Sichuan Basin

D The Yangtze Plain

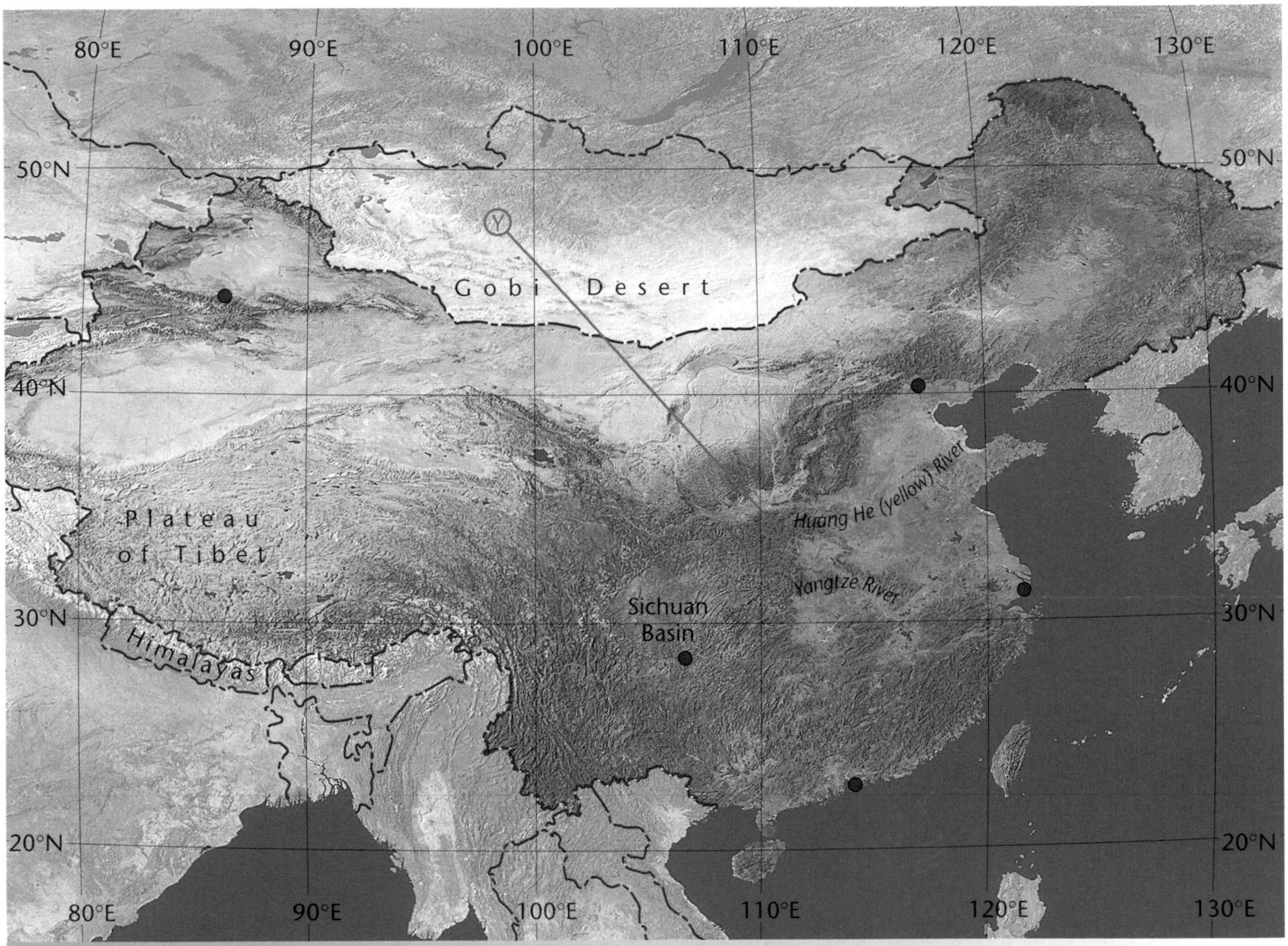

E **A satellite image of China**

ACTIVITIES

1 a) Use an atlas to make a list of the countries on China's borders.

b) Use the scale in your atlas to measure the distance across China at its widest point from west to east, then north to south.

c) Compare your results with maps of **(i)** the UK and **(ii)** the USA.

2 a) You will need an outline map of China. Use the satellite image **E** and an atlas to mark on the regions referred to in the text.

b) On your map, label the definitions of each of the following: plateau, river basin and plain.

3 a) From satellite image **E**, identify the three physical regions along latitude 30°N.

b) From information on the photographs **A**, **B** and **D** and cross-section **C**, describe the type of landscape in each of the three physical regions.

4 a) Write a description of the main landscape features you would pass over if you travelled along transect line X—Y in the satellite image **E**.

b) Choose another transect line of your own. Describe the features you would see if you travelled along it.

5 Use an atlas to identify the five cities at the following co-ordinates on the satellite image **E**: 40°N, 117°E; 32°N, 122°E; 23°N, 114°E; 28°N, 108°E; 44°N, 87°E

6 Compare and contrast China's physical geography, as summarised on these two pages, with that of any other country you have studied. Use the following headings to help you:

- relief;
- main physical regions;
- main rivers.

China's contrasting climates

- ▶ How and why does the climate vary across China?
- ▶ How does the climate affect people's lives?

Similarities and differences of climate

Much of inland China has a **continental climate**, with extremely cold, dry winters and hot, wetter summers. However, China is a very large country so the climate varies enormously from place to place (**A**). Some of the main factors to influence China's climate are:

- the south is hotter because the sun is at a higher angle in the sky, so it heats the ground more intensely;
- the west is mostly mountainous and it gets colder at higher altitudes due to the lower air pressure;
- the coast is wetter since air blowing from the sea tends to pick up more moisture than air blowing from the land;
- the south is also wetter because warmer air can hold more moisture;
- winds blowing from the north of China bring colder air than winds from the south.

Beijing		Jan	Feb	Mar	Apr	May	Jun	Jul	Aug	Sep	Oct	Nov	Dec
	Precipitation (mm)	4	5	8	17	35	78	243	141	58	16	11	3
	Temperature °C	-5	2	5	14	20	25	26	25	20	13	4	-3

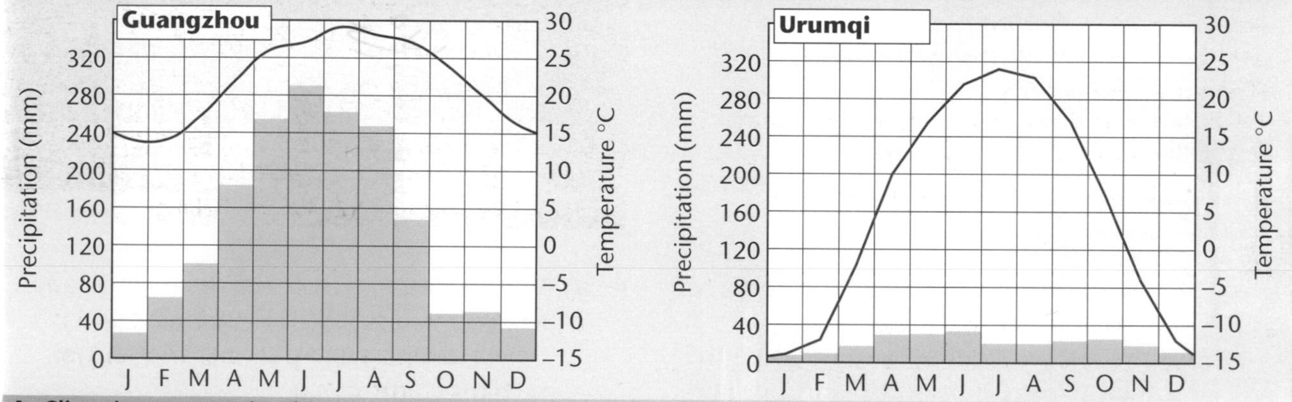

A Climatic contrasts in China

How air masses affect the seasons

Air masses are large areas of the atmosphere where the temperature and humidity of the air is fairly uniform. The air masses get these characteristics from the area where they form and they change as they move away from this source area. Diagram **B** shows the usual situation in the winter.

In summer, the winter pattern is reversed. The land mass heats up and air rises to create low pressure (a depression) over the north. This draws air in from the warm seas to the south and east. Summer is warmer and wetter, particularly in the south. The hot summer days here lead to rapid **convectional uplift** of hot air, and result in frequent, violent thunderstorms.

How climate affects the people

The climate has a huge impact on many aspects of people's lives wherever they live. Farming is obviously affected by the climate, but so are features like building design, communications, energy supply and demand, leisure activities, and many other aspects of our way of life. Every year thousands of Chinese are killed by extreme weather events such as floods, blizzards, typhoons, hailstorms and droughts. Recent examples include:

- 50 killed by a powerful sand storm in Xinjiang;

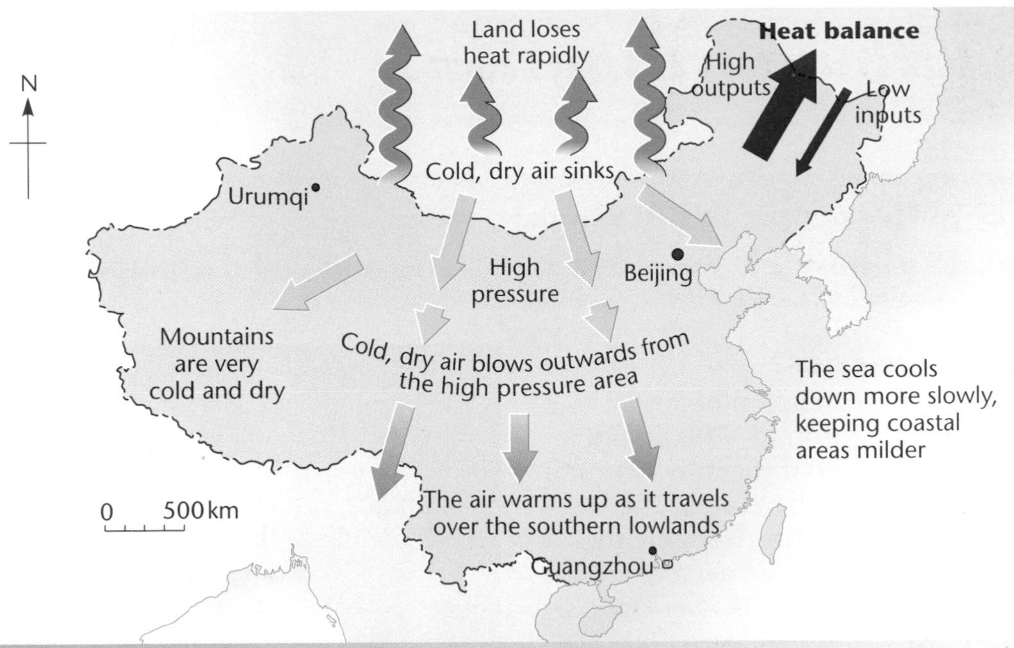

B Effects of the anticyclone over northern China in winter

- hailstones up to 8cm in diameter in Hunan killed 9 people and destroyed crops;
- 600 killed in traffic accidents after snowstorms in Beijing;
- 103 000 trapped by snow in remote Xinjiang Mountains;
- 14 killed and 42 injured when lightning hit a building in Guizhou province;
- 1 200 killed in flooding of the Yangtze River.

C Snow over the Imperial Palace, Beijing

ACTIVITIES

1 List five ways in which the weather has affected your way of life recently.

2 a) Draw an outline map of China. Label the main factors that influence the climate.
b) List three reasons why some places are warmer than others.
c) List two reasons why some places are wetter than others.

3 Look at diagram **B**. Use the text to draw a similar diagram for the situation in the summer.

4 What are the pressure and wind patterns in:
a) a depression?
b) an anticyclone?

5 Look at the climate graphs for Guangzhou and Urumqi.
a) Describe and explain the differences in:
- the temperature patterns and annual temperature ranges;
- the rainfall patterns and annual totals.

b) Draw a climate graph for the Beijing figures given in the table in **A**. Account for the climate your graph shows.

6 Which time of year would be the best to organise the following activities:
a) an outdoor football competition in southern China?
b) a white-water rafting trip in the interior?
c) a visit to the Great Wall, north of Beijing?
Give reasons.

7 Try to find out about a recent weather hazard in China. Explain what happened and how it affected people.

Population distribution

▶ Where do the people live in China?
▶ What factors have influenced that pattern, and will it change?

How many are there?

China has the largest population of any country in the world at around 1200 million people. About 900 million of them live in rural areas and 300 million in urban areas. The country covers 9.6 million km^2 (roughly the same size as the USA), giving an average **population density** of 130 people per km^2. Some regions of the country, however, have a far higher population density than others.

A A high density location

B A low density location

Low density regions

The western part of China has about 10% of the population living in 60% of the land area. Some areas have fewer than 1 person per km^2. Some of the reasons for the low population density are shown in diagram C.

High density regions

The highest population densities have always been found in the eastern lowlands. Here the floodplains have fertile soils and longer **growing seasons**. Even in the drier areas the rivers can often be used to irrigate farmland.

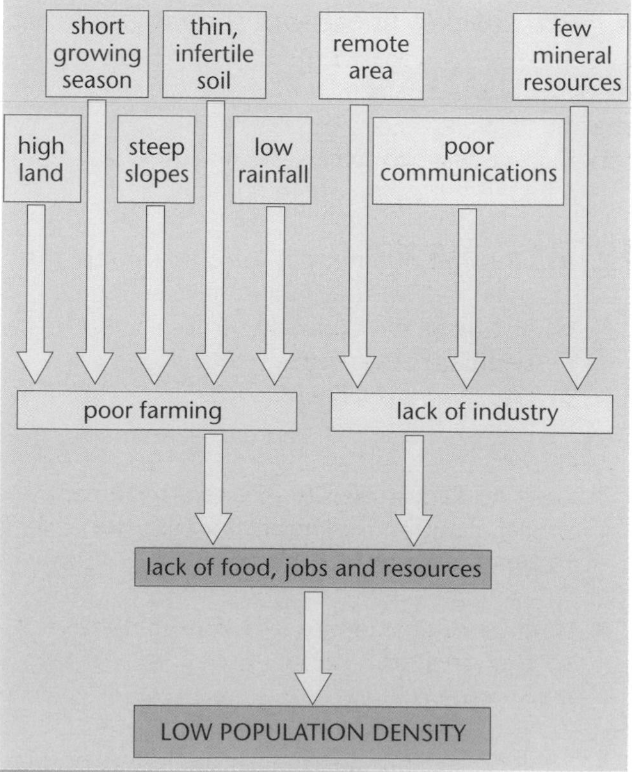

C Reasons for a low population density

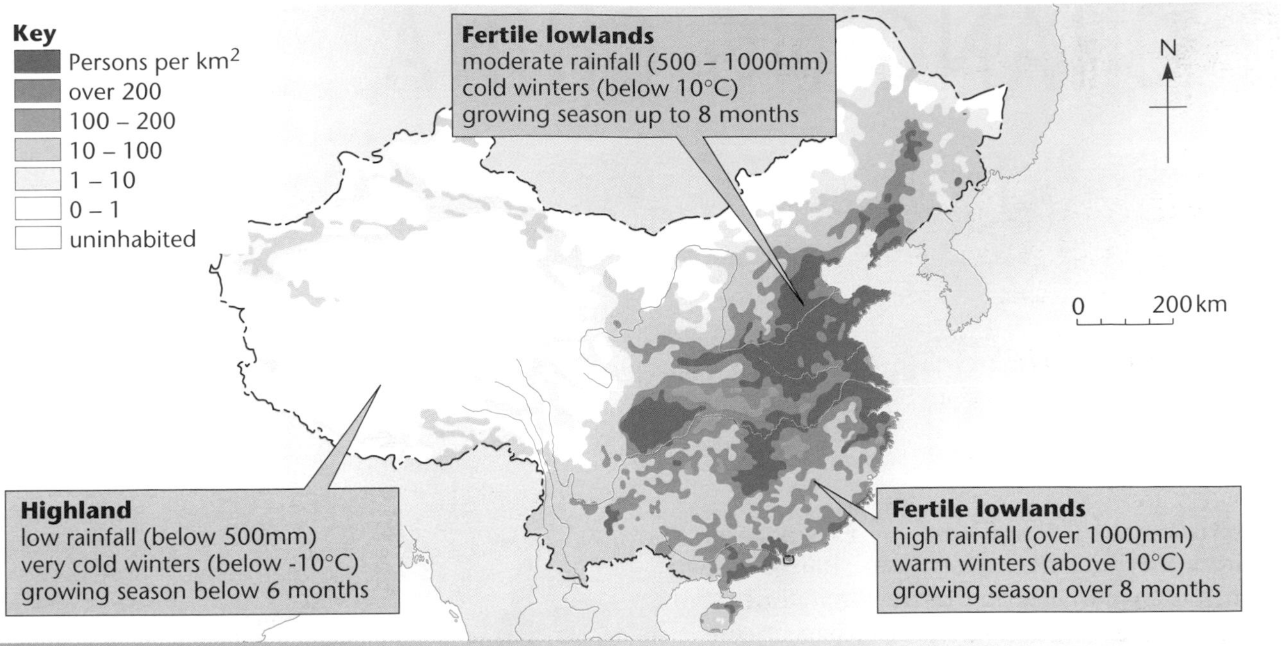

D Population density of China

Administrative and commercial cities are found throughout China. Most of the industrial cities of China are in the north-east where important mineral resources, such as iron ore, coal and oil, are found. Industries such as iron and steel, chemicals, motorcars and textiles have developed using these raw materials and energy.

The **accessibility** of the eastern region is another reason for its higher population density. Trade by ship has led to the growth of many large ports like Tianjin, Qingdao, Shanghai and Hong Kong along the coast of China. There are also more railways, roads and inland waterways in the east of the country.

Government influence

In the 1950s many people moved from the crowded cities to remote rural areas. Until recently each person was registered in one place and was not allowed to move elsewhere without permission. This system has now been relaxed and there are thought to be about 100 million '**floating workers**' who have moved from the countryside to the cities to look for work. Unless the government makes rural life more attractive, the pattern of **population distribution** may become more uneven in the future.

ACTIVITIES

1 What is meant by the terms:
a) population density?
b) population distribution?

2 Look at diagram **C** showing the reasons for low population density in western China.
a) Draw a similar diagram for the east of the country using the information given in the text.
b) Using atlas maps, suggest other factors that affect the population distribution.

3 Why does the climate have such a big influence on the distribution of population in a country like China?

4 a) In your atlas, find a population distribution map for the UK. In what ways is the pattern of population distribution in China similar to the pattern in the UK?
b) In what ways is it different?

5 75% of China's population live on 15% of the land area.
a) Show this situation as clearly as possible in some form of sketch or diagram.
b) What problems might arise as a result of the pattern shown by your diagram?

2 CHANGING CHINA

Population structure and growth

▶ How does the population of a country grow?
▶ How is the structure of China's population changing?

Arrivals and departures

The population of a country can change in two ways. One way is through 'the conveyor belt of life', where births add to the numbers at one end and deaths remove people at the other. By subtracting the number of deaths from the number of births you can calculate the rate of natural increase of population in the country. The other way that the population may change is by people leaping off and on the conveyor belt to and from other countries. These movements are called **international migration**.

A How the population changes

China's growth spurt

China's population has grown very slowly for most of its history. Although the **birth rate** was high, so was the **death rate**. Even as recently as 1950 people's **life expectancy** in China was only 40 years.

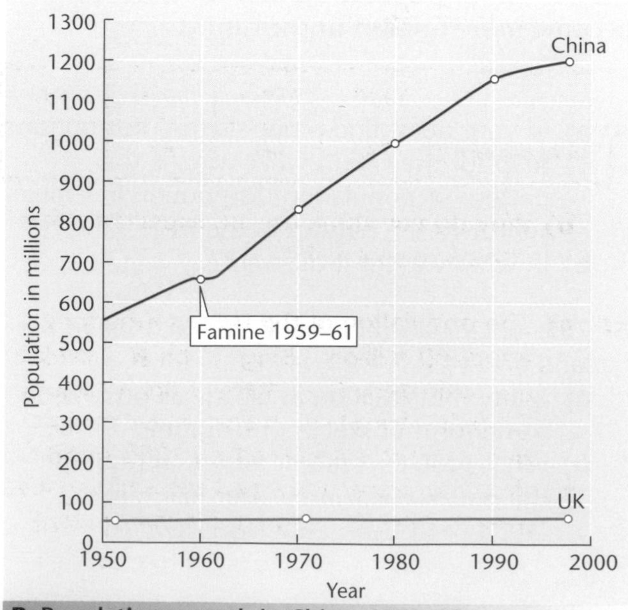

B Population growth in China, 1950–98

It took around a thousand years for China's population to double from 50 million to 100 million. It took only forty years for it to double from 500 million to 1 000 million. After the Communists gained power in 1949 they encouraged population growth. As living conditions improved and the **death rate** fell, the population began to grow alarmingly and by the 1960s the authorities were encouraging birth control.

Population pyramids

A population pyramid is a useful diagram to show how the population is divided among males and females of different ages. The shape of the pyramid can tell what is happening to the population. High percentages at the bottom of the pyramid show a high birth rate. A rapid narrowing of the shape towards the top means a high death rate in the country. A war, famine or mass emigration will show up as a 'dent' in the shape of the pyramid.

China's 'greying' population

China's birth and death rates have fallen and the life expectancy has risen. This means that the proportion of older people in the country is rising. Many countries are worried about the effect that this might have on their economy. The elderly are often seen as a drain on resources, although the main problem may be that these countries have not made plans for the changing age structure of their population.

C Elderly card players in Fujian

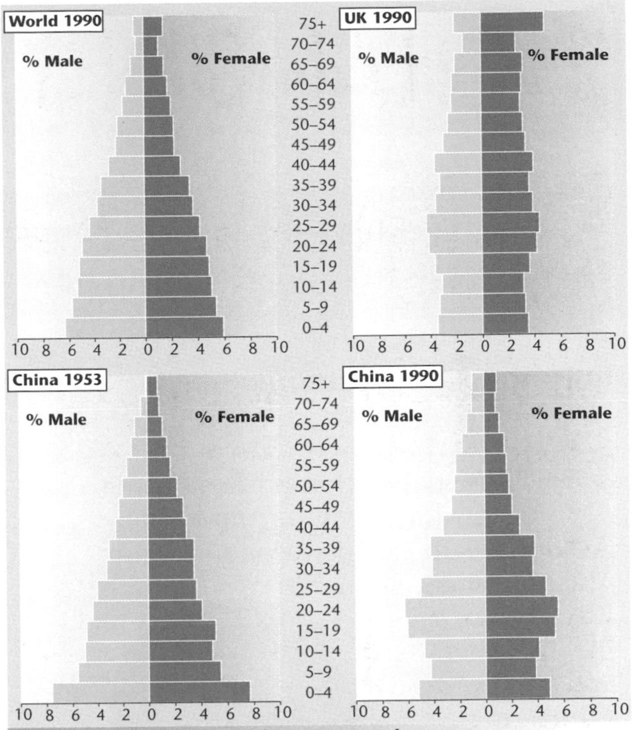

D Population pyramids compared

ACTIVITIES

1 Draw a diagram or explain in your own words the two ways in which the population of a country can change.

2 a) Copy and complete the table below of birth rates, death rates and natural increase for China.

Year	Birth rate (per 1000)	Death rate (per 1000)	Natural increase (per 1000)
1950	44	25	19
1970	31	9	22
1990	18		11
1997		7	10

b) Describe what the figures show you about China's population.

3 a) Describe China's population growth since 1950 as shown on graph **B**.

b) What are some of the reasons for the growth shown?

4 Look at the population pyramids **D**.

a) How has the shape of China's pyramid changed since 1953? What does this tell you?

b) What similarities and differences are there in the shape of the UK and China pyramids for 1990?

c) Sketch what you think the shape of China's pyramid might be like in 40 years time.

d) Outline some of the problems that China might face because of their 'greying' population.

e) In what ways might elderly people be seen as a benefit to a country?

5 a) Draw a graph or pictogram to represent the changes in life expectancy as shown by these figures.

Year	1930	1950	1970	1997
Life expectancy	24	40	63	70

b) Why do you think the life expectancy has improved so much?

6 a) The population of the United Kingdom is about 60 million. Using graph **B**, calculate approximately how many years it took China's population to add on 60 million people after it had reached 1000 million.

b) What are some of the positive and negative aspects of such rapid population growth?

Crowd control

- ▶ Why has China introduced population policies?
- ▶ What are these policies and how successful have they been?

How many are too many?

"If the population problem is not dealt with, it will be impossible to ensure healthy economic and social development"

Zou Jiahua, Vice-Premier.

The number of people living in an area is usually related to the resources that are available there. People have basic needs, such as food, water and shelter, which they get from the environment. Some environments are rich in resources and will support many people, while others will support very few.

Population policies

In the 1970s couples were encouraged to marry later, to leave at least four years between births and to have only two children. This was replaced by a one-child policy in the 1980s. The aim was for zero population growth – a balance of births and deaths – by the year 2040. The policy is not a law, but there are incentives for parents who follow the aim and penalties for those who do not.

Rural and urban differences

In the rural areas the policy was strongly opposed and couples were allowed to have a second child if the first was a girl. Traditionally, boys have been valued more highly than girls since they keep the family name while girls join another family through marriage. Cases of female **infanticide** have been reported and

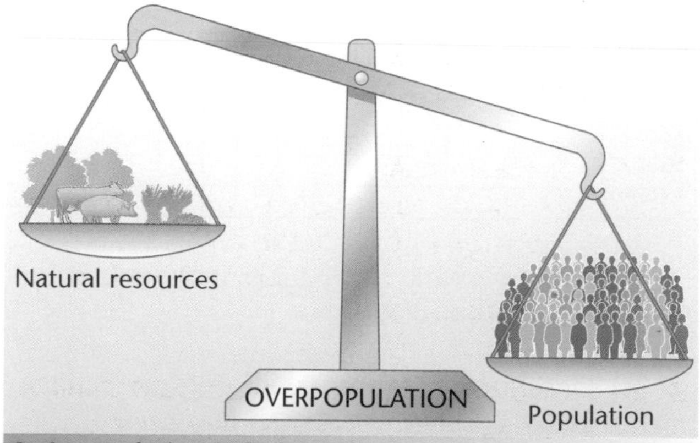

A A population imbalance

Incentives for one-child families:
- financial rewards
- free schooling
- free medical provision
- government jobs, housing and pensions.

Penalties for second pregnancies:
- fines (often a year's salary)
- no more free schooling nor medical care
- pressure to undergo abortions or sterilisations
- loss of government jobs, housing and pensions.

many births are simply not recorded. Tests to determine the sex of unborn babies are now officially banned.

The policy has been more widely accepted in urban areas where people are less traditional. City populations are more educated than those in the countryside and women are more likely to follow careers. Space is limited and an extra child has a greater influence on the family's standard of living.

B A "little emperor"

Success or failure?

"China's efforts to control population growth proved to be successful, with a population 200 million less than what it could have been had nothing been done," according to the Chinese government.

A typical family now has four grandparents and two parents devoting all their attention to one child (referred to as the 4-2-1 system). These children, easily spoiled and increasingly overweight, are called "little emperors and empresses". There has been a rise in juvenile misbehaviour, crime and violence recently and many blame the change in family structure for making the young Chinese expect more attention and success.

ACTIVITIES

1 What do you think Zou Jiahua means by his statement?

2 Look at diagram **A**:

a) How could the scales be made to balance?

b) Will a large population in an area always mean that it is overpopulated? Explain your answer.

3 a) Why did the Chinese government think that it needed some sort of population control in the 1970s? (Also look at the graph on page 12 and explain your answer.)

b) Present these figures as a graph or a pictogram:

Year	1963	1980	1998
Average number of children per woman	7.5	2.3	1.8

4 a) Produce a government advertisement in support of the one-child policy. This could be a poster, leaflet, radio script, television advert or internet page.

b) What arguments might be raised against your advert by civil rights groups or other opponents?
You might write a protest letter from such a group or organise a class debate on the issue.

5 a) What does the government say would have happened with no population policy?

b) How has China's population policy changed the shape of its population pyramid (see page 13)?

c) Why might it take 30 years or more for population policies to have any real effect on the numbers?

6 Find out about the population policies of other countries. Are there any countries that are trying to persuade their citizens to have **more** children?

A country on the move

- ▶ **What is the pattern of migration within China?**
- ▶ **Why do people move? How does this change affect their lives?**

A large number of people are moving within China. In 1995, at least 100 million people were living in a different province from the one in which they were born. This migration has occurred mainly since 1984, when the communist government began to allow people to move more freely. At least four out of every ten migrants have moved from rural to urban areas.

Push factors
In the rural areas:
- the amount of agricultural land is decreasing;
- farming is being modernised;
- there are few job opportunities.

Therefore many people are without land, jobs or income.

Pull factors
In the urban areas:
- there are many new construction, manufacturing and service industries;
- more jobs are created;
- higher wages are available;
- there is more housing.

Therefore there is a growing demand for workers.

Map **A** shows which of China's provinces have gained and lost population because of internal migration. The population of many of the provinces of eastern China has increased rapidly because the government has encouraged industries in **Special Economic Zones**. For example, as a result more than a million **migrants** were attracted to Guangdong Province between 1985 and 1990 (Map **D**). Zhuhai was one of China's five Special Economic Zones set up in the early 1980s (Extract **C**).

A Population change caused by internal migration, 1985–90

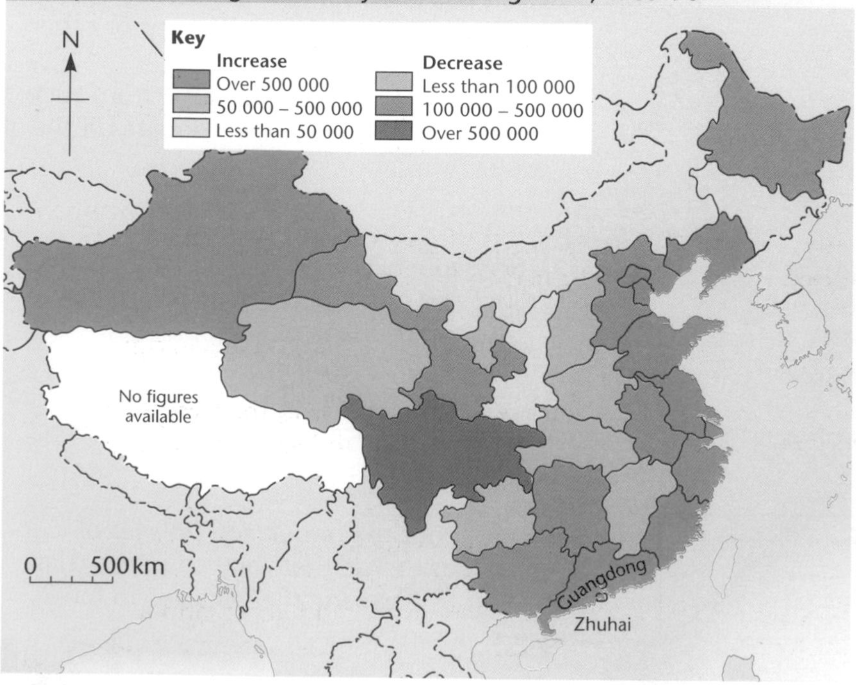

B Migrant women in Zhuhai

Migrants flock to Zhuhai

In the harsh midday sun, Zhuhai's Jida industrial estate is a cheerless concrete expanse with row upon row of factories. But come dusk, it is transformed into a lively meeting place as vendors hawk their wares and migrant women stream out of factories to pick up their dinner. Conversations float through the air, some in Putonghua, most in dialects from nothern China.

Almost half of Zhuhai's population of 607 000 are migrant workers, and 80 per cent of them are women aged 16 to 25.

The economic zone has a special lure for these women, many of whom move there to escape the bleak work prospects back home. Especially at a time when massive layoffs are taking place at state-owned companies throughout the mainland, Zhuhai is viewed as a land of opportunity.

Tan Shen, a senior researcher at the Chinese Academy of Social Science, estimates there are four million migrant women concentrated in the Guandong boomtowns of Dongguan, Zhongshan, Shunde, Shenzhen and Zhuhai. She says the economic success of these cities is largely due to the female migrant labour force.

"These girls who work in joint-venture factories, restaurants or hair salons, as servants of hawkers, are mostly from Sichuan, Hunan, Guangxi and Jiangxi," says Ms Tan, adding that the northern provinces, whose economies developed later than those in the south, have surplus labour.

While many in the north can make money only during the harvest, in Zhuhai they have a steady income.

"Once they've worked in the south for three or four years, the cleverer ones will go back with their savings and start a village enterprise," says Wang Xiulin, editor of China Women's News. "They can be hair stylists or open a clothing shop."

But not everything is as rosy as is it seems.

"The girls may have adjustment problems when they come to the big cities. They work long hours and have little social life.'

Extract from *South China Morning Post*, 29 March 1998

C Zhuhai province: push and pull

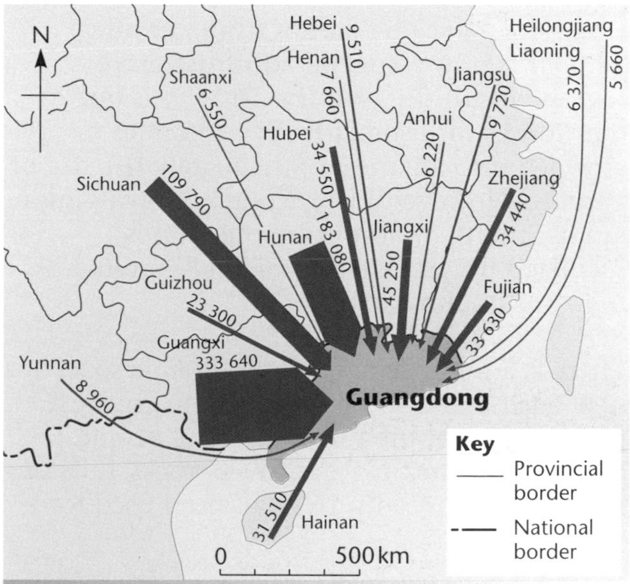

D Migration to Guangdong from other parts of China, 1985–90

ACTIVITIES

1 Explain, in your own words, what is meant by push and pull factors.

2 Study map **A** and the map on page 5.
- **a)** Name three administration regions that lost most people through migration.
- **b)** Name three administration regions that gained most people through migration.
- **c)** Name the administration region on map **A** for which no information is available. Suggest why this might be the case.

3 Study map **D**.
- **a)** Describe the pattern of migration to Guangdong.
- **b)** Suggest reasons for the pattern you have described.
- **c)** From the information on page 51, explain what is meant by a Special Economic Zone.
- **d)** Explain how Special Economic Zones affect population distribution in China.

4 Study extract **C**.
- **a)** Why do you think a large percentage of the migrants to Zhuhai are young women?
- **b)** Design a Guangdong Provincial Government advertisement aimed at attracting young women to Zhuhai from the northern provinces.

5 Liu Yaping is a young person who left Sichuan to work in Zhuhai for two years. She then returned to her province. Using the information in extract **C** and photograph **B**, write an imaginary account explaining:
- why she left Sichuan;
- her life in Zhuhai during the two years;
- why she returned to her home province.

6 Compare and contrast the pattern of migration into Guangdong with that of another region in the world you have studied. Include maps, facts and figures, and a paragraph that summarizes the main points.

Making space in Hong Kong

- Why does Hong Kong need more economic and living space?
- What are the advantages and disadvantages of land reclamation?

Hong Kong became part of China in June, 1997. It is now a **special administrative region** within the country. The city is one of the world's most prosperous economies crowded into an area approximately the size of London. However, Hong Kong is growing more rapidly than London. Its population is predicted to increase from 6.7 million in 1999 to 8.2 million by 2016.

There is a huge demand for economic space for new businesses, and living space to ensure a good quality of life for Hong Kong people. Much of the area is either steep, rocky hills or marshland, and only 16% has been used for building on.

One solution has been to create very high density for business and housing. Another has been land reclamation. Since 1945 almost 6000 hectares of land has been developed by this means.

An example of land reclamation has been the infilling of Victoria Harbour which is surrounded by Hong Kong's central business district. The proposal to build Kai Tak City would reduce the size of Victoria Harbour even further. As with many other major urban planning schemes, the proposal is receiving much opposition.

A Extract from the *South China Morning Post*

Plan for Kai Tak City unveiled

4 September, 1998

A $36 billion plan to build a "city within a city" at the former Kai Tak airport site was unveiled yesterday.

Housing for 320 000 people, 90 000 permanent jobs and the SAR's largest urban park will be created on the 579-hectare site, more than half of which is to be reclaimed from the harbour. The four-stage development will take 18 years to complete and will see the building of 118 000 flats with roads, shops, government and school buildings, a hospital, godowns and recreational areas.

The 50-hectare Metropolitan Park is intended not just for new residents and people living in Kwun Tong and To Kwa Wan who do not have enough open space, but for people from throughout Hong Kong and international visitors.

There will also be a waterfront promenade running the length of the development, an international-standard sports stadium, a transport museum and an aviation "academy" to mark Kai Tak's past, as well as two new trunk roads and a possible railway line. Some industrial areas bordering the site will be rezoned as residential to improve the area.

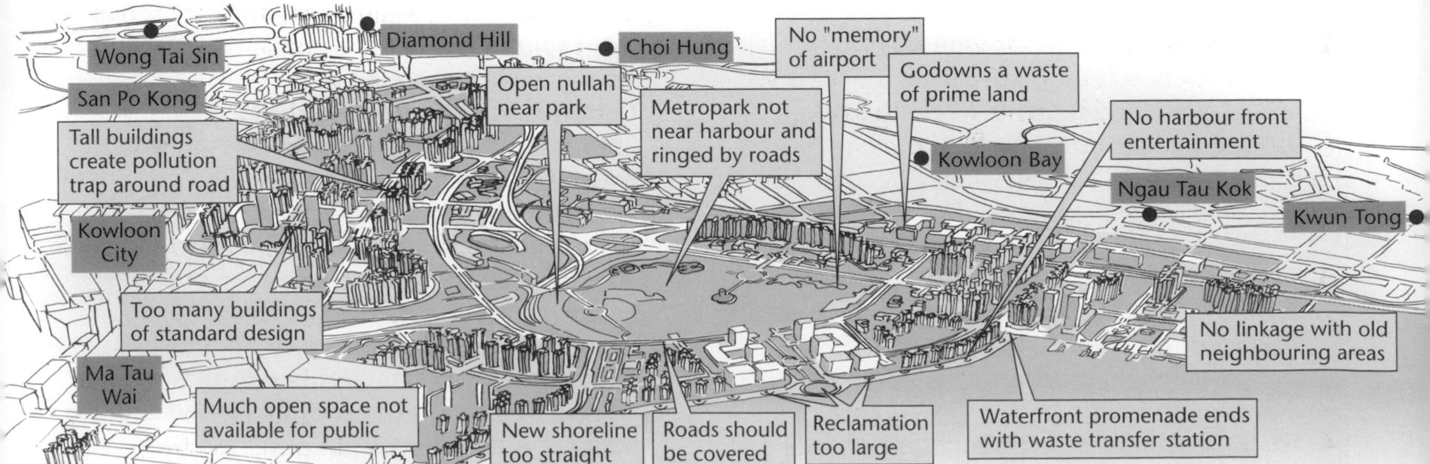

B Design for Kai Tak City in 2016: what the critics say from the *South China Morning*

C Victoria Harbour, 1964

D Victoria Harbour, 1997

E Some views of the supporters of further reclamation in Victoria Harbour

- Reclamation can provide 'natural' growth of nearby urbanised areas. Existing service and transport networks can be extended.
- These types of schemes can be completed quite quickly.
- Publicly owned land is created.
- In these central areas the value of this land is high.
- When the infill is taking place it creates a site for public dumping.
- Reclamation schemes can get rid of polluted areas of confined water like the Kowloon Bay **Nullah**.

F Some views of the opponents of further reclamation in Victoria Harbour

- There will be less water, more buildings and therefore more people; this will increase water pollution.
- Victoria Harbour is being spoilt as a world famous tourist attraction.
- The dredging carried out during reclamation causes sediment to be suspended in the water. This affects the Harbour's ecosystem.
- There will be an increase in road traffic in these already congested coastal areas.
- As this busy Harbour gets narrower, it will become more dangerous for shipping.
- Heavy vehicles carrying infill material will cause traffic and environmental problems.

ACTIVITIES

1 Write a definition of the following: economic space, living space, central business district and ecosystem.

2 a) Suggest two reasons why there is a problem about the availability of space for business and housing in Hong Kong.

b) Explain one way in which the city has tried to solve its problem of lack of space, other than by land reclamation.

3 Design a leaflet for the Hong Kong Government's Planning Department to illustrate the advantages of the Kai Tak City Plan. If possible, use a computer to help you.

4 a) From photograph **C**, trace the coastline of Victoria Harbour in 1964.

b) Trace the new coastline onto the same map from photograph **D** and shade to show the additional land reclaimed by 1997.

c) Use your map to estimate the percentage amount of land reclaimed in the 33 years.

5 Divide into groups of five for a role-play exercise. Decide which members of the group should act the following roles: an ecologist, a civil engineer, a secondary school geography student, a leading businessman and a ship's captain. Decide whether or not further land reclamation should be allowed in Victoria Harbour, using information from these two pages.

Shanghai: China's future Manhattan?

▶ How might the development of Shanghai's Pudong Economic Zone help to transform the city into becoming once more one of the world's major financial centres?

A Shanghai's skyline

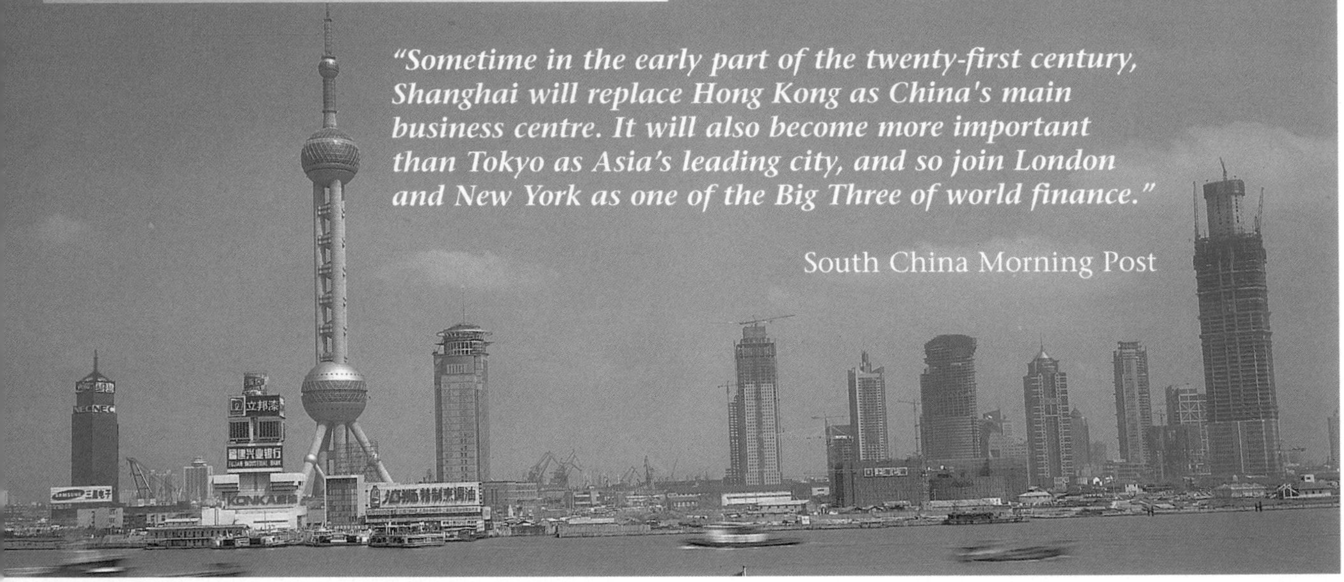

In 1936 Shanghai was the seventh largest city in the world. At that time it benefited from being one of China's five **open cities**, which meant that it traded with western countries.

After the People's Republic of China was established in 1949, Shanghai declined as a city. It only began to flourish again after 1978 when the country adopted a more open policy towards the outside world.

Two major planning schemes have been undertaken to develop Shanghai:

- the creation of **satellite towns** to decentralise the city centre and to encourage new industries;
- the establishment of the Pudong New Area since 1990. This is a previously relatively undeveloped site of 35 square km, immediately opposite the Bund, Shanghai's central business district.

The Pudong is being developed with the following main aims:

- to encourage foreign investment. Overseas firms which establish here have all the benefits of China's Special Economic Zones, as well as opportunities to deal through foreign banks located within the Pudong.
- coordination with Shanghai's congested central area to solve the city's chronic urban problems.

The development of the Pudong is an important step in re-establishing Shanghai as a major world city. The area also has strategic importance for China, because its growth should stimulate the development of the Yangtze River region as a whole.

Percentage share		
	1990	2000
GNP	8.1	25.0
Retailing	4.0	30.0
Population	10.4	14.8

B Pudong's increasing share of Shanghai's wealth and population

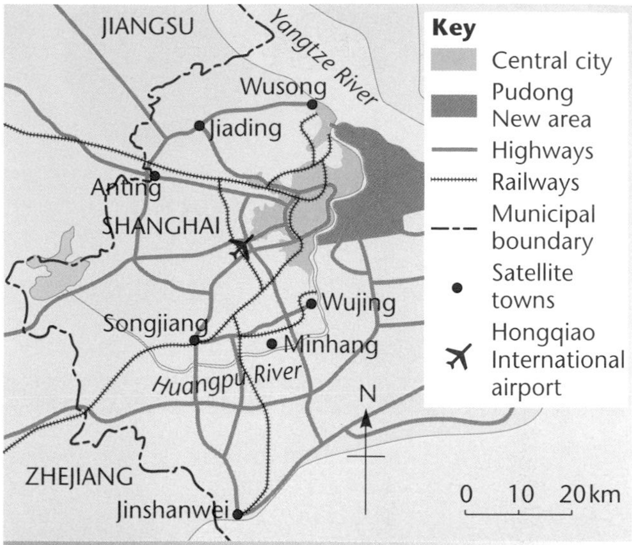

C The location of Pudong in Shanghai

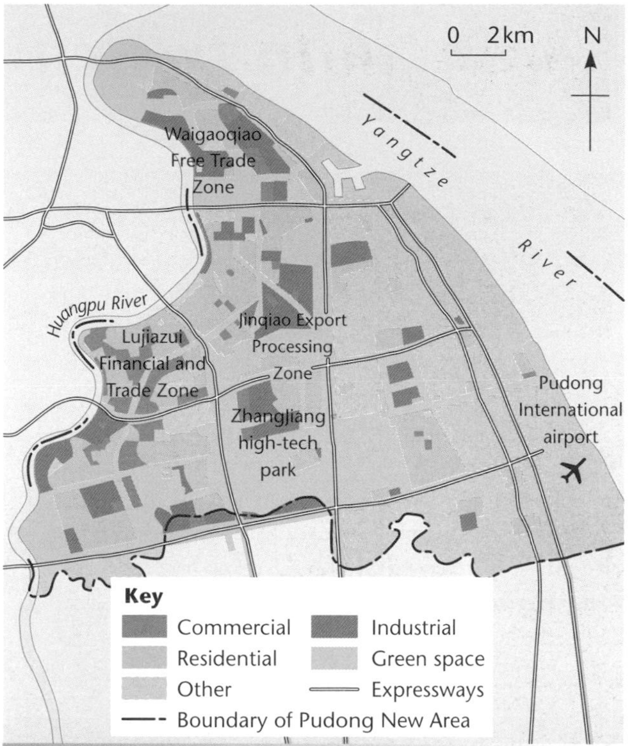

D A land-use map of Pudong

	1990	2000
GNP (RmB million)	6 020	50 000
Primary sector (RmB million)	220	500
Secondary sector (RmB million)	4 590	24 500
Tertiary sector (RmB million)	1 210	25 000
Exports (US $ million)	570	6 100
Population (million)	1.34	1.80

E The planned growth for Pudong, 1990 – 2000

- Jinqiao Export Processing Zone – export processing industries. Areas will be reserved for industries relocated from the city.
- Lujiazui Financial and Trade Zone – finance, commerce and tertiary industries, and extension of the Bund.
- Zhangjiang high-tech park – high-technology industries and universities.
- Waigaoqiao Free Trade Zone – export processing industries, warehouses, port.

F Functions of Pudong's Special Development Zones

ACTIVITIES

1 Define each of the following terms: open city, satellite town, high-tech industry.

2 Study the map of China on page 5 and suggest two advantages of Shanghai's location.

3 Explain why photograph **A** illustrates that the Pudong can be described as "China's Future Manhattan".

4 Calculate the percentage growth in Pudong's primary, secondary and tertiary sectors between 1990 and 2000, as shown in table **E**.

5 The owner of a UK computer firm wishes to locate a branch factory in Shanghai. She is offered two sites: in Songjiang satellite town and in Zhangjiang high-tech park. Working in pairs, write a consultant's report for the owner, advising her on the advantages and disadvantages of each site. Use information from these two pages.

6 Compare and contrast the Pudong with an urban planning scheme in another country you have studied.

Tailback in two cities

- ▶ What transport problems face cities like Beijing and Hong Kong?
- ▶ What solutions are being considered?

Hong Kong

Hong Kong is a city with major transport problems, as shown by photograph **A**. Despite a very efficient public transport system, the vast volume of traffic on the roads has led to increasing congestion, accidents and air pollution. It was estimated that in 1996 traffic jams caused 124 million working hours to be lost, costing the economy £1.5billion or 2% of Hong Kong's GDP (see also pages 18 and 19).

B Increasing car ownership

Year	1948	1958	1968	1978	1988	1998
Private cars	5 758	24 378	69 062	142 049	178 234	359 694
Total vehicles	10 051	35 305	109 654	233 150	347402	569 411

C Average daily passenger journeys

1997	Bus	Train	Taxi	Car	Tram	Ferry
Number (1000s)	5 787	3 281	1 298	1 081	291	196
%	48	27	11	9	3	2

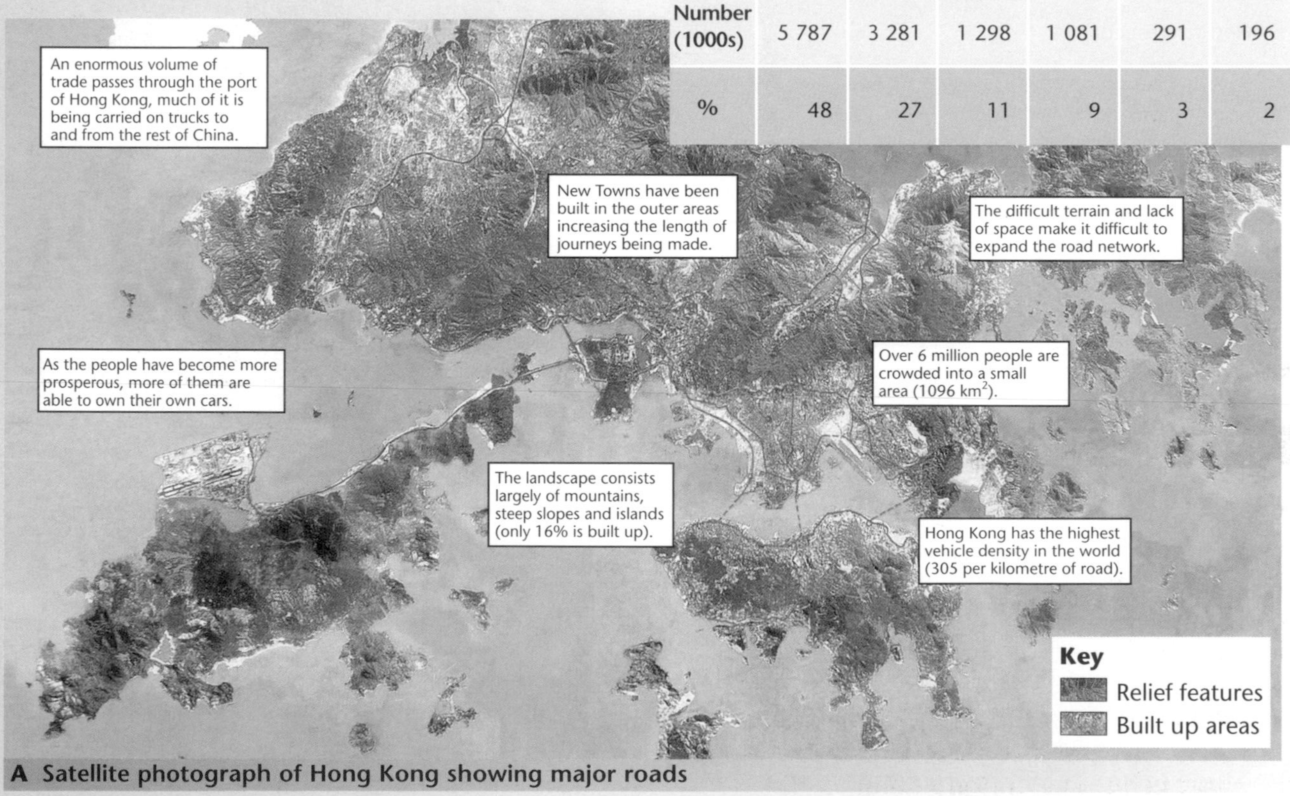

A Satellite photograph of Hong Kong showing major roads

Strategies considered, or already in use, include:

- bus only lanes (localised only, so not really effective);
- staggered working hours and working from home;
- higher charges at some toll tunnels to encourage motorists to use less congested routes;
- 40% extension of the railway system;
- park-and-ride schemes from railway stations in the outer areas;
- higher road tax, fuel tax and registration fees;
- restrictions on the number of new car licences;
- an Electronic Road Pricing scheme (ERP), where motorists pay to use busy stretches of road.

Beijing

Beijing has not always had the traffic problems that you would expect in a city of over 12 million people. In 1985 private cars in the city were virtually unknown. Cycling is said to be about 20% quicker and more comfortable than the overcrowded public buses and trains in the rush hour. However, as more people can afford a car, the usual problems of congestion and pollution are increasing, with the added issue of conflict between cars and bicycles on the major roads.

D Cyclists in Beijing

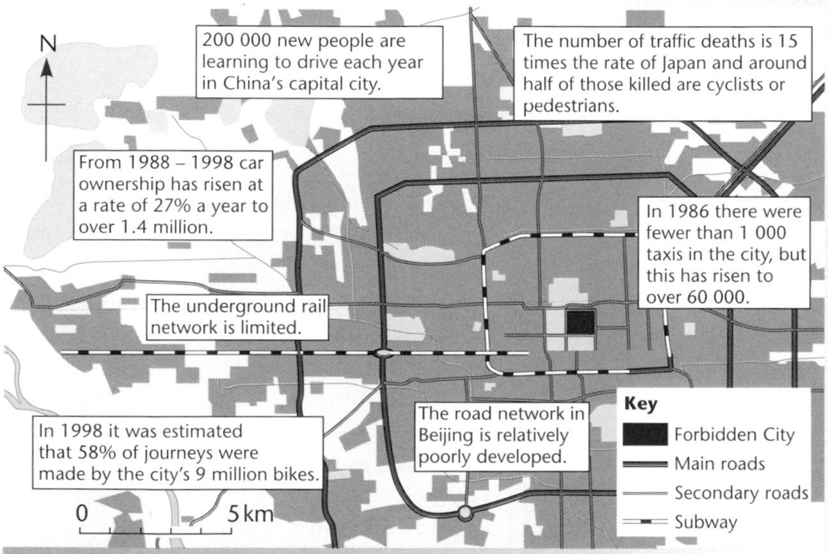

E Road and rail map of Beijing

Strategies considered, or already in use include:

- encourage greater use of public transport, rather than bicycles;
- ban bicycles from busy sections of road from 7 - 8 am;
- remove lines of trees that separate bicycle lanes from car lanes on many routes;
- build four ring roads to speed up traffic flow;
- ban odd or even numbered vehicles on certain days of the week;
- transport more cargo at night;
- get more people to observe traffic regulations.

ACTIVITIES

Work in a group to produce a report on the traffic problems and solutions of Hong Kong and Beijing. Organise your report into sections and add illustrations wherever possible. You might include the following:

1 A table of the transport problems of the two cities. Use these three columns in your table:
- Problems only in Hong Kong
- Problems only in Beijing
- Problems in both cities.

2 Presentations of at least four pieces of data for each city in graphs, pictograms or other graphical forms.

3 The advantages and disadvantages of each strategy shown in the text for the two cities, and your group's opinion of how effective it might be.

4 An annotated sketch map of each city showing the strategies that your group would recommend.

5 An explanation of any extra ideas that you have added, not from the text.

6 A summary of your plan for each city.

7 Do some research to find out how other major cities of the world are trying to overcome their transport difficulties. (Hong Kong Transport Department: http://www.info.gov.hk/td)

3 CHALLENGE OF THE ENVIRONMENT

China's sorrow

- What causes a river to flood, and what damage can be done?
- What can people do to reduce the risk of flooding?

Flooding on the Yellow River

The Huang He, or Yellow River, is the second longest in China (over 5000 km long). The river has flooded in three out of every four years in the past, causing widespread destruction and thousands of deaths. In both 1889 and 1938, it is thought that flooding killed almost one million people. No wonder the river is also known as 'China's sorrow'.

Why does it flood?

The river floods when it cannot carry all of the water and the **load** in its channel. The flow of water into the river comes from precipitation and melting snow in the drainage basin. The load is mostly made up of fine, yellow soil, called **loess**. Each year the river washes away about 1.6 billion tonnes of soil from the drainage basin. Look at diagrams **B** and **D** for further information.

MAY	Snow melts in the mountains. The wet season begins.
JUNE	River level rises and bursts its banks in 8 000 places. Plans are made to evacuate 876 000 people.
JULY	1 million local people work to strengthen the defences. An estimated 8 million people affected; 5 million hectares of farmland are submerged.
AUGUST	End of the wet season. Estimated deaths 2 500 and economic losses £12 billion.

A A typical wet season (1996)

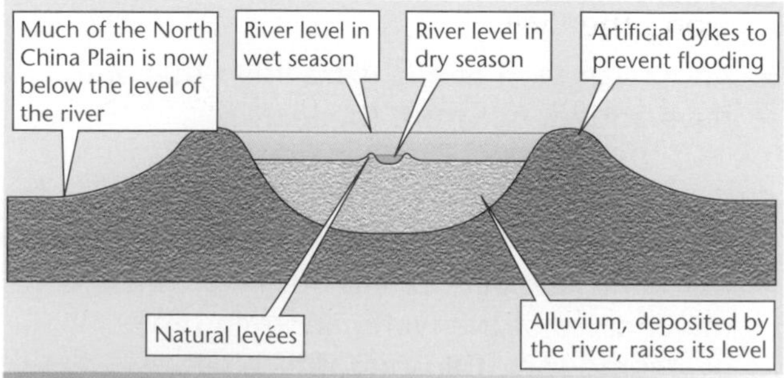

B Cross-section of the river in its lower course

C Dykes on the Yellow River help prevent flooding

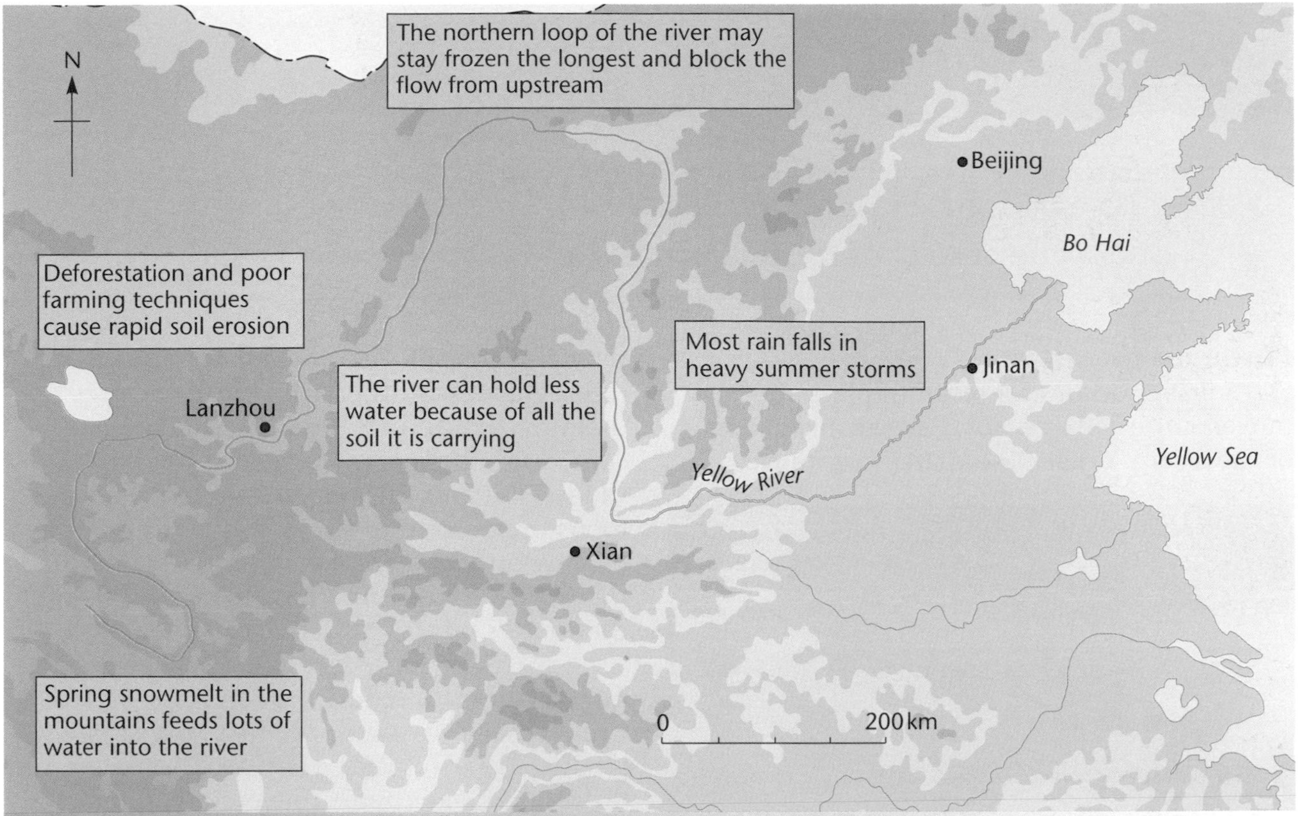

D Some causes of flooding on the Yellow River

Flood management

In the past the people relied on **dykes**, built along the sides of the river to prevent flooding. Widespread tree planting is now being encouraged and the farmers are using **terraces** on the steeper slopes. Both of these measures slow down surface flow and reduce **soil erosion**.

Many dams have been built along the river and its **tributaries** to hold back water in the flood season. They also provide water and **hydro-electric power** for people, farms and industry. Navigation is also improved as the river is deeper in the dry season.

The river has been straightened and dredged in many places to speed up the flow of the water to the sea.

ACTIVITIES

1 Why is the Huang He also known as **a)** China's Sorrow and **b)** The Yellow River?

2 When is a river most likely to flood?

3 Look at diagram **D**:
- **a)** Put the causes of flooding shown on the map into two lists under the headings of natural factors and human actions.
- **b)** Explain how human actions have increased the chances of flooding.

4 a) In diagram **B**, explain how the river got to be higher than the North China Plain.
- **b)** Why is this so dangerous?

5 Draw a sketch map, similar to map **D**. Annotate the map to show the measures that have been taken to try to reduce flooding along the river.

6 a) Read the information about the 1996 floods. Devise possible newspaper headings for three dates during the floods. Write the first paragraph for each of the articles.
- **b)** Why might the Chinese government be concerned about the flooding of the Huang He?
- **c)** Describe the feelings of a peasant farmer whose entire farm has been flooded.

Broken China?

▶ Why do earthquakes occur in China?
▶ What are the results of these earthquakes?

Plates on the move

Earthquakes occur as a result of plate movement, the large, solid, jigsaw-like pieces of the earth's **crust**. Two plates may move slowly past each other for centuries. As they rub against each other, friction may cause them to stick and the pressure then builds up. Sometimes the rocks free themselves with a sudden jolt and this releases energy from the **focus** in the form of shock waves. China is not directly on a known plate boundary, but it has many active **faults** and has suffered some of the world's most destructive earthquakes.

Year	Location	Magnitude (if known)	Deaths
1556	Shansi, China	–	830 000
1976	Tangshan, China	8.0	655 000
1737	Calcutta, India	–	300 000
1138	Aleppo, Syria	–	230 000
1927	Xining, China	8.3	200 000
856	Damghan, Iran	–	200 000
1920	Gansu, China	8.6	200 000
893	Ardabil, Iran	–	150 000
1923	Kwanto, Japan	8.3	143 000
1290	Chihli, China	–	100 000

A Most destructive known earthquakes on record, (USGS National Earthquake Information Centre)

Earthquake prediction

Chinese scientists were the first to accurately predict an earthquake. They monitored ground distortions, water table movements, small tremors and animal behaviour. On 4 February 1975, the **seismologists** informed the government that a quake was due near Haicheng. Later that evening, after over 1 million people had been evacuated, there was a **magnitude** 7.8 earthquake. The China Daily newspaper recently reported that 18 out of 24 earthquakes were correctly forecast in a study that measured the rise in temperature of the earth's crust, from satellites.

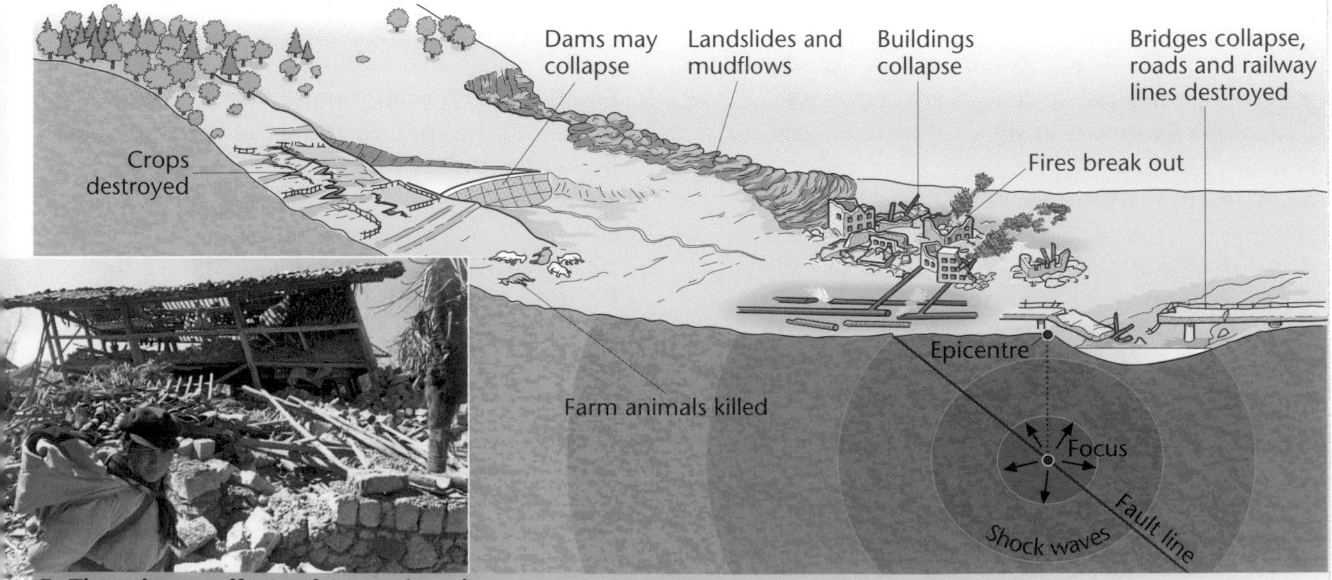

B The primary effects of an earthquake

The destruction of Tangshan

Unfortunately, the massive earthquake which destroyed Tangshan in July 1976 was not predicted. The city lies next to a fault line that runs through northern China and was flattened by a magnitude 8.0 earthquake. It is thought that around 655 000 people were killed (China puts the number at 250 000). Several factors contributed to the high loss of life:

- the **epicentre** was directly beneath a densely populated area;
- the city was built on soft **alluvium** which behaves like quicksand when it is shaken;
- the brick-built buildings of the city were not shake-resistant and collapsed easily;
- the quake struck at night and most victims were buried and crushed as they slept.

The summer heat and heavy rainfall that followed the quake brought problems as diseases spread through the refugee camps. It was days before relief agencies could get water, food, medicine, clothing and shelter to the survivors. These threats to life that follow the actual earthquake are called secondary effects.

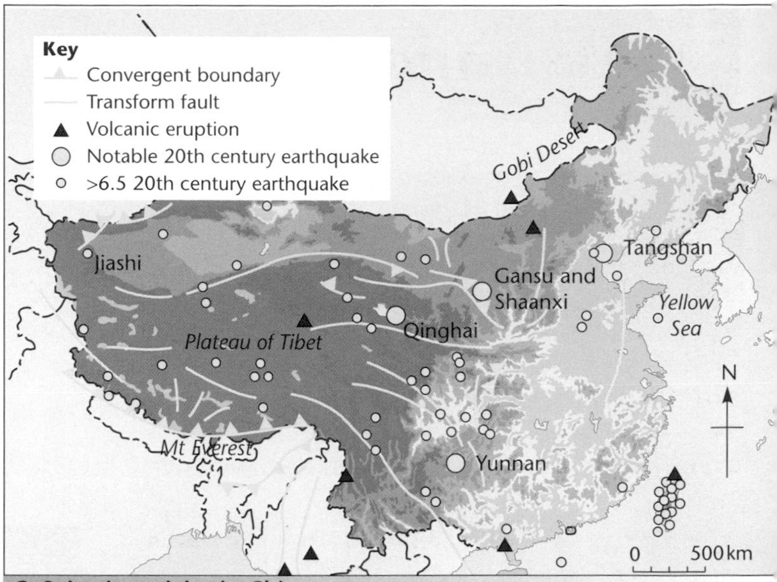

C Seismic activity in China

D — Jiashi, 24 January 1997

Two powerful earthquakes struck the Jiashi region 3 000 km west of Beijing yesterday. At least 50 people have been killed as buildings were flattened and army medical teams are treating the hundreds of injured in open-air clinics. The earthquakes measured 6.4 and 6.3 on the **Richter scale** and destroyed 15 000 houses. 2 500 families are sleeping in tents or on school floors. Reports say that 3 360 livestock animals were also killed. Officials fear that the cold winter weather (-15°C), lack of food, diseases, and difficulty getting supplies into the remote area may lead to more deaths.

Associated Press

ACTIVITIES

1 **a)** How many of the ten most destructive earthquakes in history occurred in China?
b) Why do you think so many people have been killed in Chinese earthquakes?

2 Describe how earthquakes occur. Use sketches to help you. Label them, using some of the key words from the text.

3 Draw a table with two columns. In the first column list the primary effects of an earthquake as shown on diagram **B**. In the second column list the secondary effects that might follow from each primary effect.

4 **a)** Which of the primary effects shown on diagram **B** would have contributed to the enormous death toll in Tangshan?
b) Draw a diagram to show the factors that contributed to the high death toll.

5 **a)** Read extract **D**. How do you think the conditions for the survivors of the Jiashi earthquake might have got worse in the weeks after the report?
b) How can the time of day or time of year affect earthquake hazards in different parts of the world?

6 **a)** List some of the methods used to forecast earthquakes. Try to explain each method.
b) How could the authorities make cities like Tangshan safer in future earthquakes?

7 Find out how people have tried to make it safer to live in other earthquake prone areas.

The disappearing soil

- ▶ Why is soil so important to us all?
- ▶ What is causing the rapid loss of soil in some places?
- ▶ What can be done to prevent excessive soil erosion?

The importance of soil

"The nation that destroys its soil, destroys itself."

ex-US President Franklin Roosevelt.

Soil is the layer of **weathered** rocks and decomposed vegetation at the ground surface. It is vital to all of us because it is where plants grow, and so it is where we get our food from. It takes between 200 and 1000 years to form 2.5 cm of topsoil and some of the soil is always being removed by the wind and the rain. The actions of people have increased the natural rate of **soil erosion**, so that globally about 75 billion tonnes of **topsoil** are being lost every year. It has been calculated that this loss of soil costs over £250 billion a year, or nearly £50 for every person on earth.

A A typical soil profile

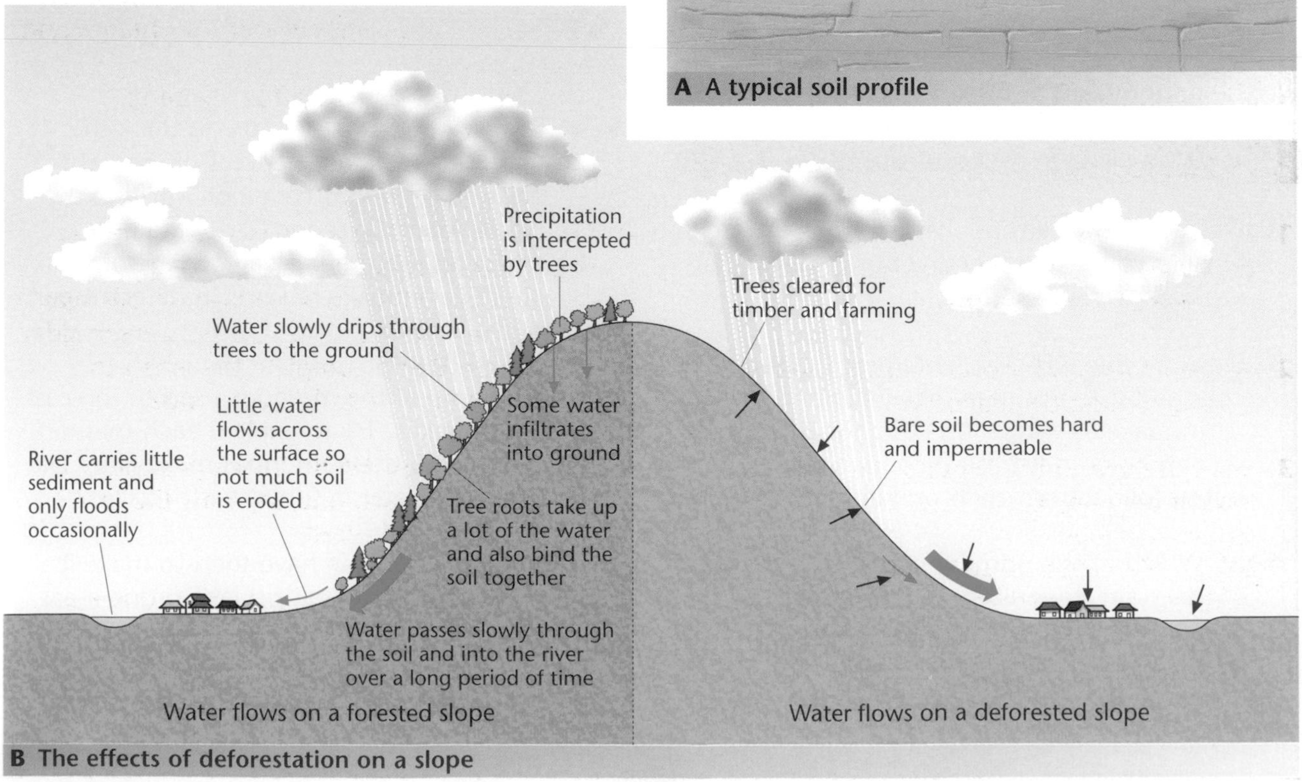

B The effects of deforestation on a slope

The situation in China

China is losing about 30-40 tonnes of **topsoil** per hectare per year, with only about 1 tonne per hectare being formed. It is estimated that the losses of nutrients through soil erosion are nearly the same as the amount of fertilizer that the country produces each year.

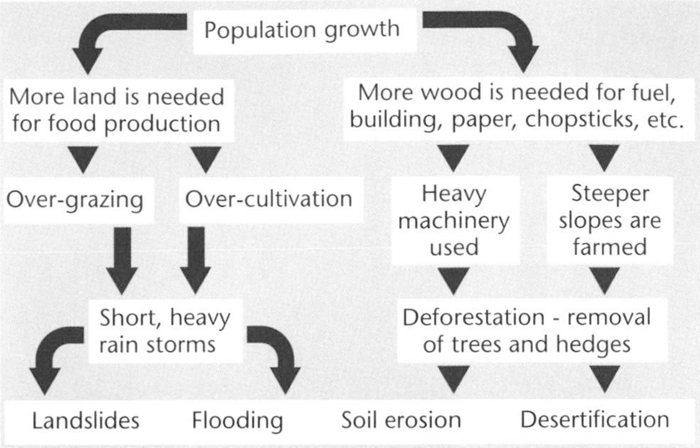

C How the problems arise

D Terracing increases yields and helps reduce soil erosion

Losing the loess

The Loess Plateau is a region along the Yellow River, about the size of France and with a similar population. Loess is the name of the fine, silty, fertile soil of the area. The soil holds little water in the dry climate and is easily eroded by wind and water, particularly if the steeper slopes are farmed. It is claimed that when farmers are working on the Loess Plateau, the increased dust in the air can be detected in Hawaii, 5000 km away.

The World Bank project

The **World Bank** is assisting China in a project to increase agricultural production in the area and to reduce the amount of soil being lost into the Yellow River (about 1 billion tonnes a year). The project will:

- take 100 000 hectares of the most vulnerable land out of cultivation;
- plant 270 000 hectares with grass, shrubs or trees, depending on the conditions;
- terrace 83 000 ha of slopes between 5° and 20°. Terracing can increase yields by three times as well as reduce soil erosion by 95%;
- construct small earth dams that can hold back 90% of the water and nearly all of the soil. They also provide water for villages and for irrigation;
- provide funds for education training and research.

ACTIVITIES

1 a) What is soil?
b) What do you think Franklin Roosevelt meant by his statement?

2 Write definitions for over-grazing, over-cultivation and desertification.

3 Read the text under "Losing the loess" and look at diagram **C**.
a) What is loess?
b) List the causes of soil erosion given in these two sources under the headings of *natural factors* and *human activities*. What do your lists tell you?

4 One study found that soil erosion in forests was 0.3 tonnes per hectare per year, compared to 90 tonnes per hectare per year in unforested areas. Copy the right-hand side of diagram **B** and complete the labels to show why there is such a difference.

5 Make a list of the World Bank's project proposals. For each one, say how the local farmers will be affected.

6 Some people argue that poverty is the real cause of the erosion problems on the Loess Plateau. Why might they say this? Do you agree or disagree? Give reasons for your argument.

Is China choking?

- ▶ Why is air quality so poor in parts of China?
- ▶ What is happening as a result of this poor air quality?

Trouble in the air

In China enormous amounts of pollutants are released into the atmosphere. This can affect the health of the people and the quality of the environment. The industrial cities suffer the most, but pollution can also be carried to other parts of the country and beyond. Some gases released may increase the **greenhouse effect** and some damage the ozone layer. Others result in the problem of **acid rain**.

Cancer of the respiratory system is the biggest single killer in urban China.

Nine out of 10 of the world's most polluted cities are in China. (World Resources Institute, 1999)

The air in 90% of China's cities fails to meet the government's clean air standards.

Year	1942	1949	1960	1970	1980	1990	1995
Million tonnes	70	32	265	360	600	1 004	1 298

A Increasing coal use in China

B Many areas of China are heavily polluted

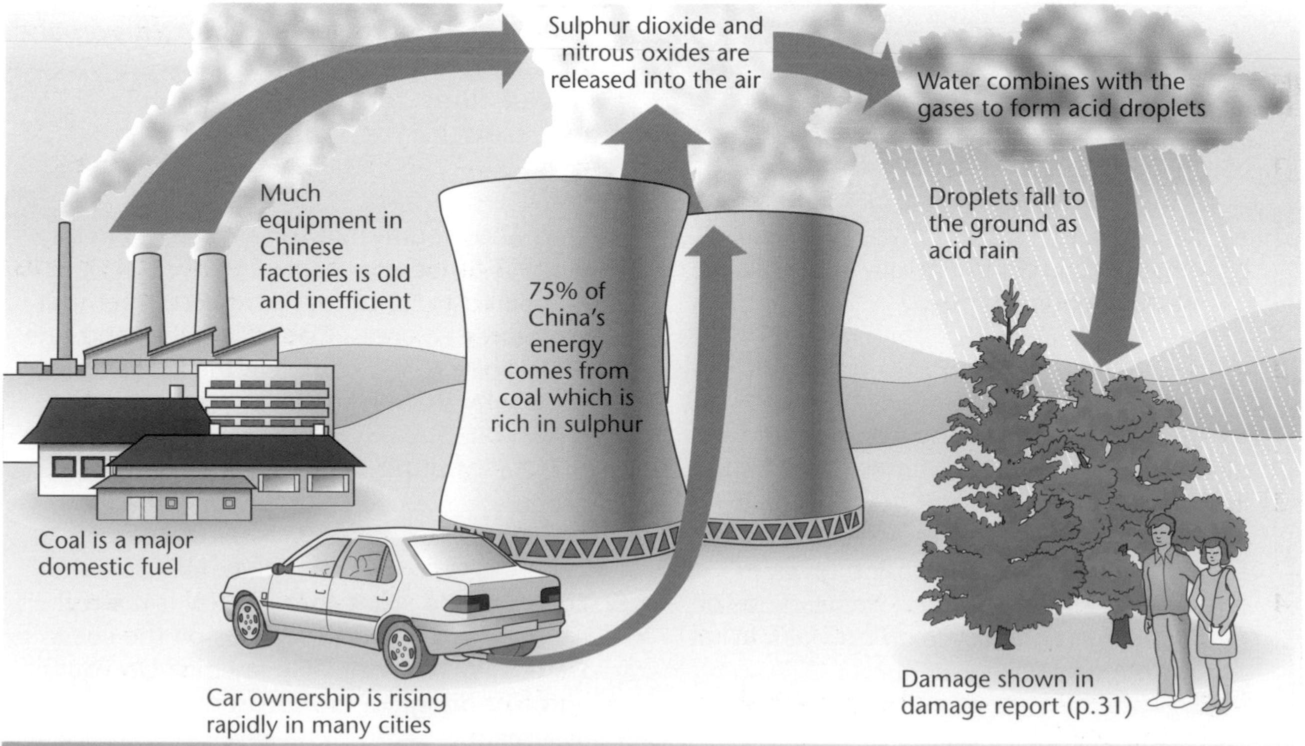

C Production of acid rain

Damage report

PEOPLE

Toxic metals dissolve into the water supply, damaging peoples' nervous system. Lung cancer and **respiratory diseases** increase.

SOIL AND PLANTS

Nutrients such as calcium and potassium are leached out of the soil. Plants, crops and trees can be damaged or killed.

WATER

Increased acidity in lakes and rivers harms fish and plant life. Fish may suffocate or be unable to reproduce.

STRUCTURES

Buildings and other structures can be corroded by the acid rain.

The worst sufferer?

PATIENTS NAME: Chongqing, in Sichuan Province
ALSO KNOWN AS: China's dirtiest city
MAIN CAUSE OF SICKNESS: emits 800 000 tonnes of sulphur dioxide into the atmosphere yearly.
SYMPTOMS:

- double the regional rate of asthma and lung cancer;
- thousands of hectares of forest destroyed;
- four species of trees have died and had to be replaced along the city streets;
- paint peels off buildings three times faster than in Beijing;
- metal railings and lamp-posts have to be frequently replaced as they corrode.

DIAGNOSIS: "Chongqing is not fit for humans to live in," according to one resident.

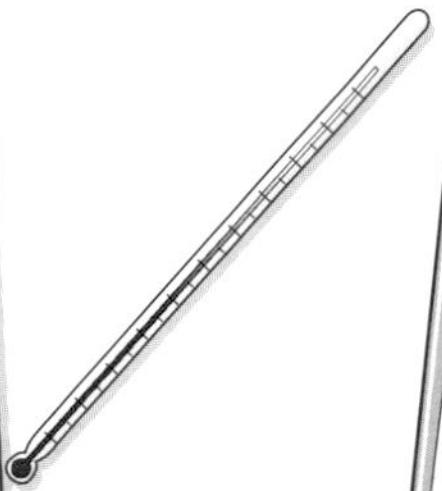

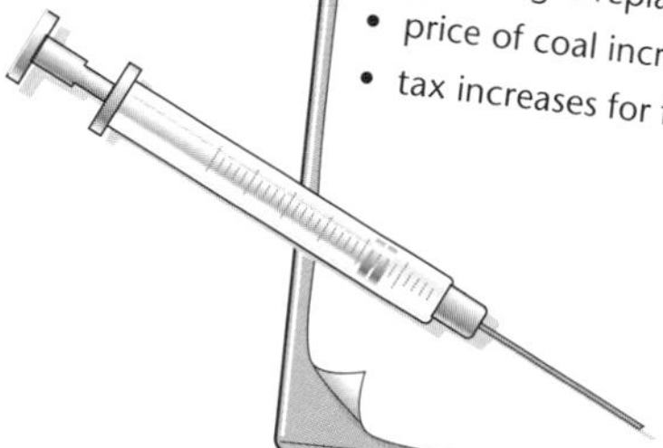

The recommended treatment?

The Chinese government recognises that there is a major problem and is taking the following steps to improve matters:

- £4 billion funding for environmental protection;
- cleaner coal introduced in some cities;
- natural gas replacing coal in Beijing;
- price of coal increased (subsides reduced);
- tax increases for factories that pollute.

ACTIVITIES

1 Study diagram **C**.
 a) Which two gases are released into the air to form acid rain?
 b) List the four sources of those gases shown on the diagram.

2 a) Which parts of China are likely to suffer most from acid rain?
 b) Give examples and explain your answer.

3 How might countries like Korea and Japan also be affected by China's air pollution?

4 a) Use the figures in table **A** to plot a graph that shows the use of coal in China from 1942 to 1995.
 b) Give several reasons for the pattern shown by the graph.
 c) What do you think might happen to the figures in the future?

5 a) Explain how the recommended treatments could help a city like Chongqing.
 b) Would you also suggest any other treatment?
 c) Explain why the Chinese government would be reluctant to reduce industry in Chongqing.

6 a) Which part of the damage report do you think is most worrying? Why?
 b) Chinese officials argue that they cannot afford the technology to reduce air pollution. How would you reply to this argument?

Development versus conservation

- ▶ How have the geographical developments on Hong Kong's Lantau Island affected the economy, the environment and the local people?
- ▶ In what ways might the area be conserved for future generations?

A Chek Lap Kok airport, Lantau Island

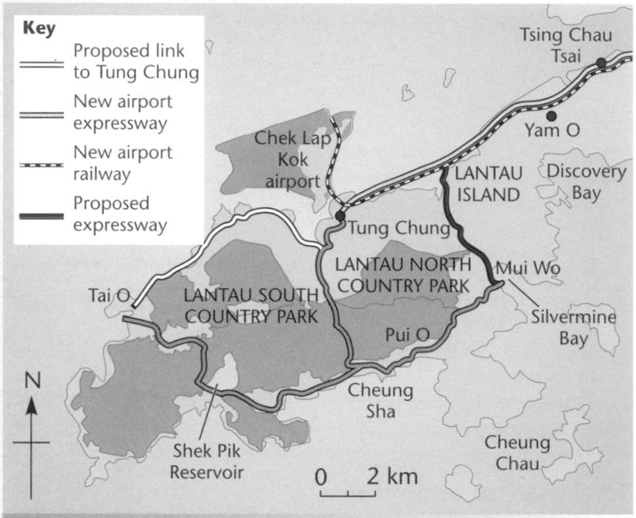

B Map of Lantau Island

Lantau Island is part of the Hong Kong Special Administrative Region. In recent years it has been transformed from a remote rural environment into a very important development area. The island is now linked to the Hong Kong mainland by a suspension bridge and expressway, a railway and a cross-harbour tunnel. One of the world's largest airports, Chek Lap Kok, was opened on Lantau in June 1998. Tung Chung New Town has been built to support the new airport. Hong Kong people have conflicting views about these new developments, summarised in diagram **C**.

C Geographical development leads to:
- economic gain and economic loss;
- environmental gain and environmental loss;
- social gain and social loss.

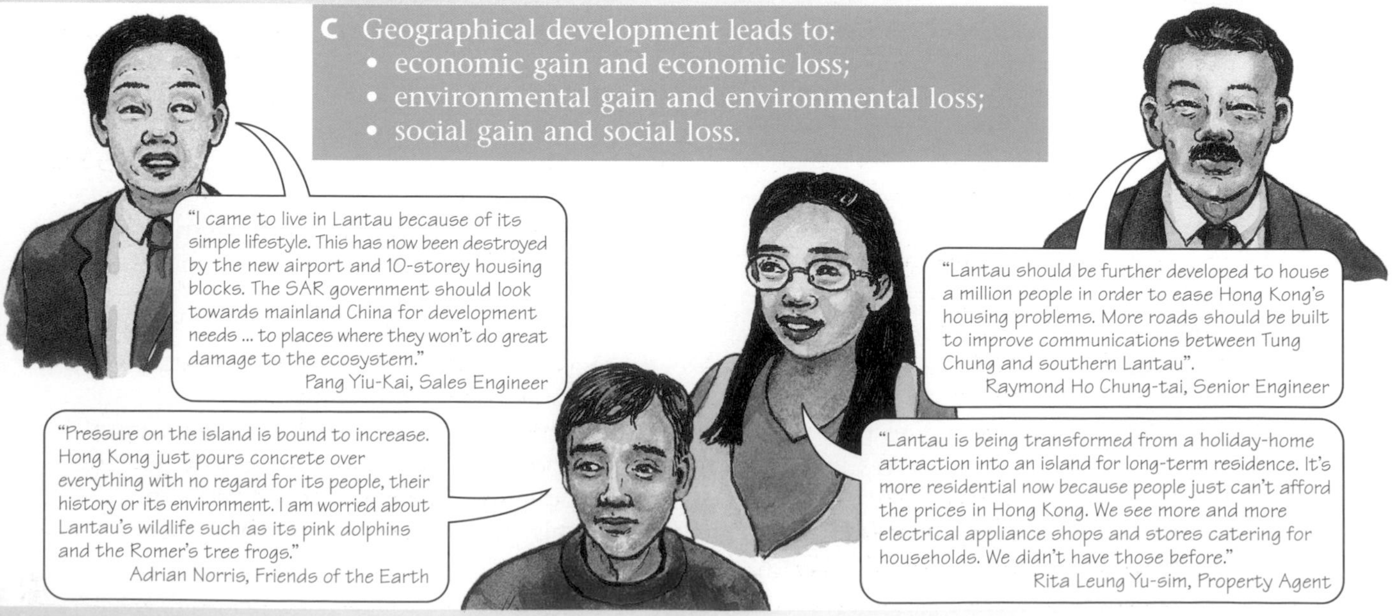

Lantau: facts and figures

- Chek Lap Kok airport has an annual capacity of 35 million passengers (11 million more than Hong Kong's former airport).
- Tung Chung New Town had a population of 20 000 in 1998.
- It is estimated that this population will rise to 200 000 by 2011.
- In the five years before Tung Chung was established (1991-1995), Lantau's population increased by 34 per cent.

Environmental groups in Hong Kong have written a report suggesting ways in which Lantau Island might be conserved in the future. The report's main recommendations are summarised in map **D**.

D Proposals for conservation

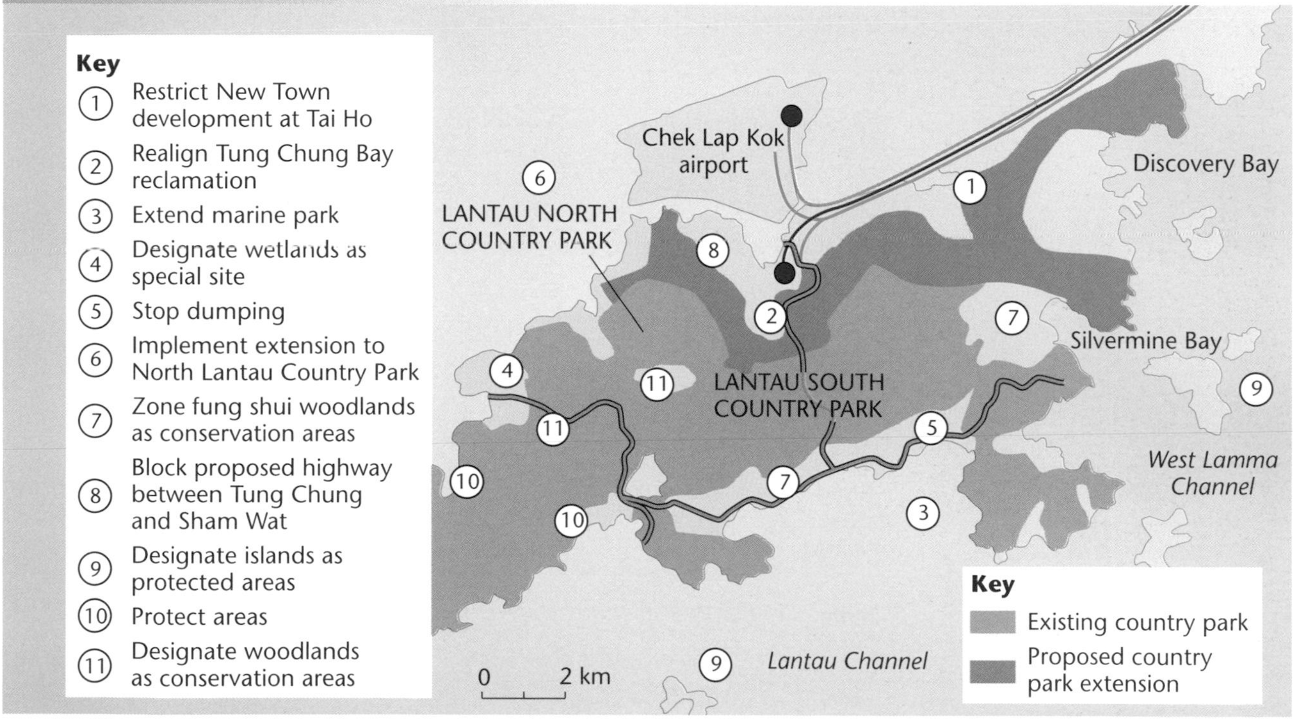

ACTIVITIES

1 a) Write definitions for the following terms: new town, country park and wetland.
b) Describe two geographical developments that have recently affected Lantau.

2 a) Study diagram **C**. Define what is meant by economic gain and loss, environmental gain and loss, and social gain and loss.
b) Draw up a table to summarise the ways in which recent geographical developments have created economic, environmental and social gains and losses for Lantau and its people. Use the views expressed by the four Hong Kong residents to help you.

3 Explain how four of the conservation measures summarised on map **D** may help to conserve Lantau's environment.

4 a) Study the sketch on page 18 that shows the site of Hong Kong's former airport, Kai Tak. Suggest why Chek Lap Kok airport is a more suitable location.
b) Write a short account giving your own views about whether or not Chek Lap Kok airport should have been built on Lantau. Use the information from the sketch on page 18 to help you.

5 From any region of the world you have studied, explain how a major geographical development has led to economic, environmental and social gains and losses. Draw up a table or write a summary of the similarities and differences of this development, compared with Lantau.

4 ECONOMIC DEVELOPMENT

China as a developing country

▶ How does China's development compare with that of other countries?

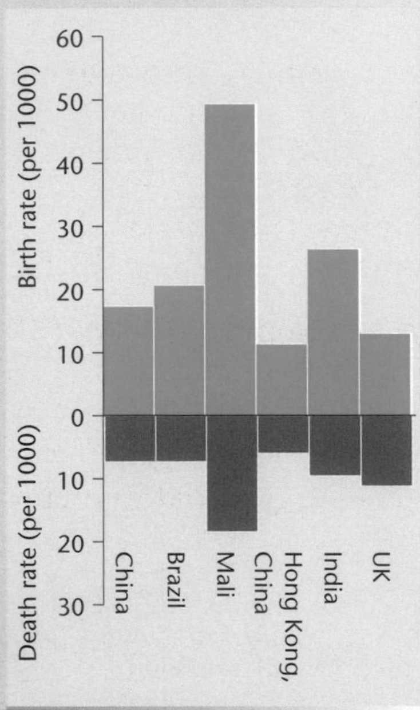

A Birth and death rates, 1995

Country	GNP $ 1995	Life expectancy at birth 1995	Adult literacy rate % 1995	Doctors per 100 000 people 1993	Secondary aged population in school % 1995	Televisions per 1 000 people 1995	Defence expenditure as % of GNP 1996
China	2 935	69.2	81.5	115	67	247	5.7
Brazil	5 928	66.6	83.3	134	45	278	2.1
Mali	565	47.0	31.0	4	9	12	1.8
Hong-Kong, China	22 950	79.0	92.2	144	75	359	3.0
India	1 422	61.6	52.0	48	49	61	2.8
UK	19 302	76.8	99.0	164	100	612	3.0

B Indicators of development

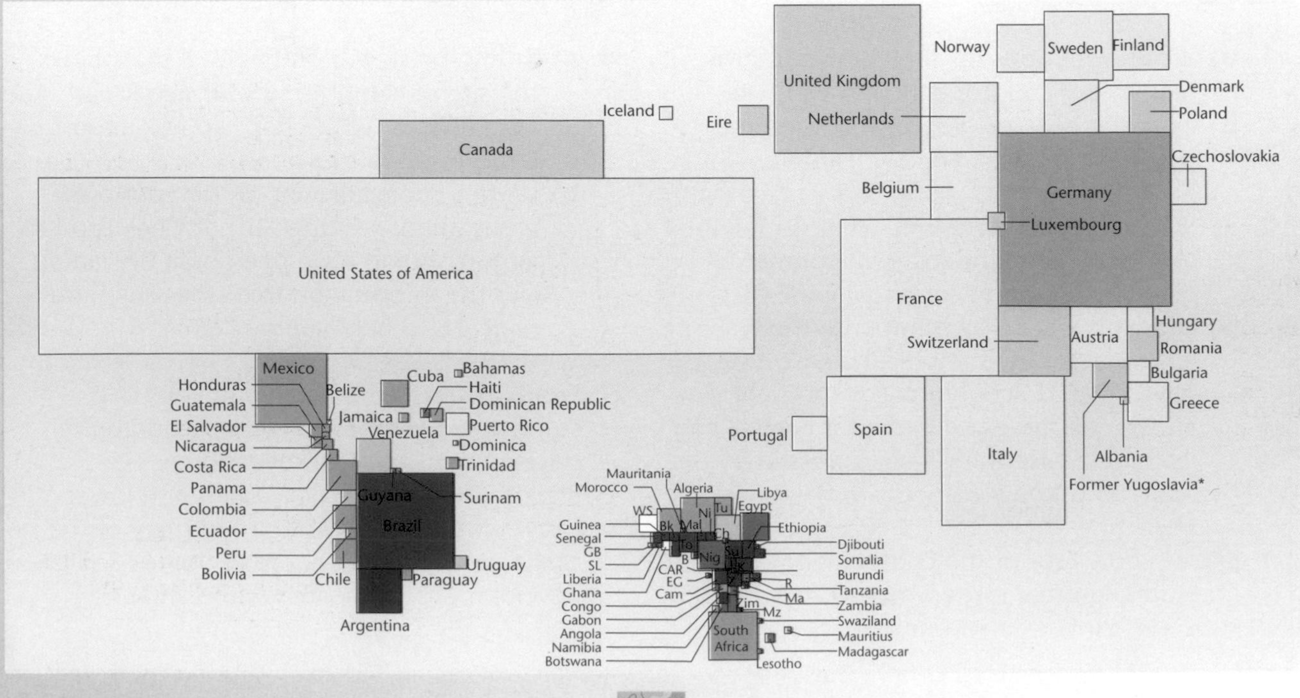

A geographical enquiry

Work with a partner during the following enquiry. Produce a joint report based on the following stages.

Stage 1 Topic for enquiry

Consider some introductory questions, for example: what is development? What is the difference between 'economic' and 'social' development?

Stage 2 Decide what data is needed and collect it

Select the relevant data from these pages and page 62. Decide what other data would be useful and use the library, atlases, the Internet, newspapers or other sources to collect the data.

Stage 3 Present your data

- Find out and explain the meaning of **GNP**, adult literacy rate, birth rate, death rate.
- Draw different types of graphs to represent the variations in the number of doctors shown in table **B**.
- Draw and complete a table to rank the six countries shown in table **B** in terms of GNP and population without access to sanitation. Draw a scattergraph from your results.
- Draw diagrams and maps to present the other data you have researched.

Stage 4 Analyse your data with reference to the topic

Analyse the graphs and other diagrams you completed for Stage 3. For example, what do they tell you about:

- China's development?
- the relationship between a country's economic and social development?

Stage 5 Draw your conclusions

- Write a few sentences to summarise your conclusions about China's development compared with that of other countries.
- Suggest two ways in which the Chinese government could increase its future economic development.

Stage 6 Evaluation

- Suggest how your enquiry could have been improved.
- What other lines of enquiry would be useful to follow?

C Percentage share of world GNP and population without access to sanitation, 1990

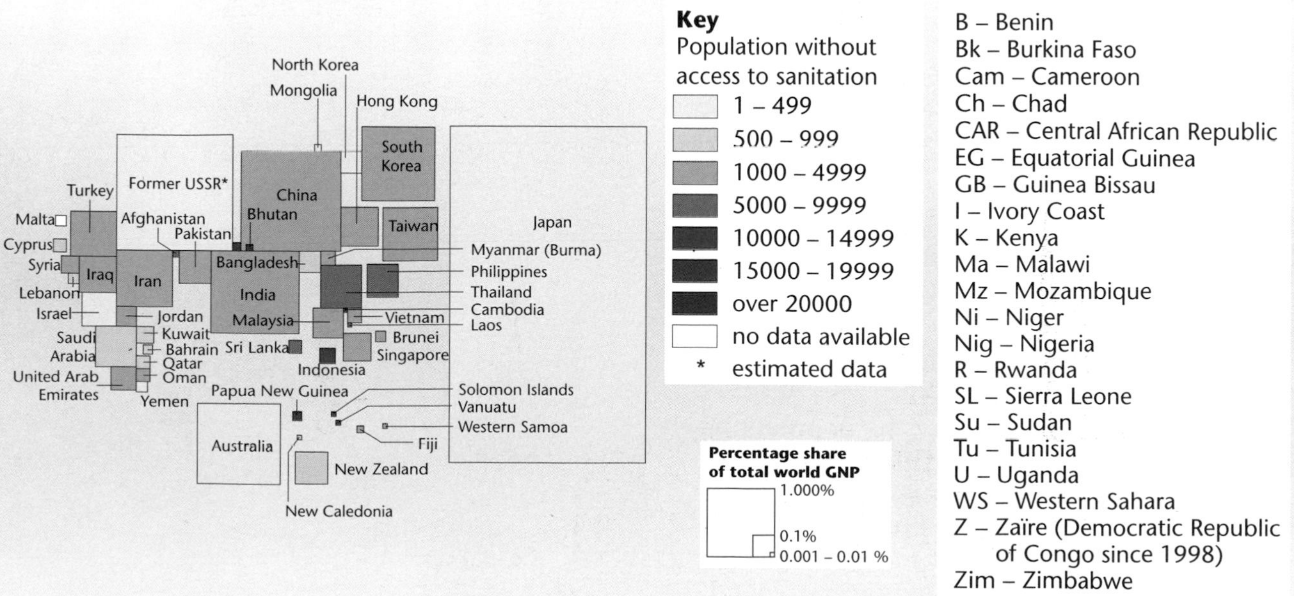

Feeding the population

- ▶ What challenges does China face in order to feed its vast population?
- ▶ How is farming in China organised?

Will there be enough to eat?

China's population has multiplied by five in the last 200 years, but only 25% more land produces food. In fact, China has lost 20% of its arable land since the 1950s and the rate of loss is increasing. Today, it has over 20% of the world's population but less than 10% of its arable land. Many people fear that a famine, like the one of 1959 – 61, in which over 30 million people starved to death, may occur again in the future.

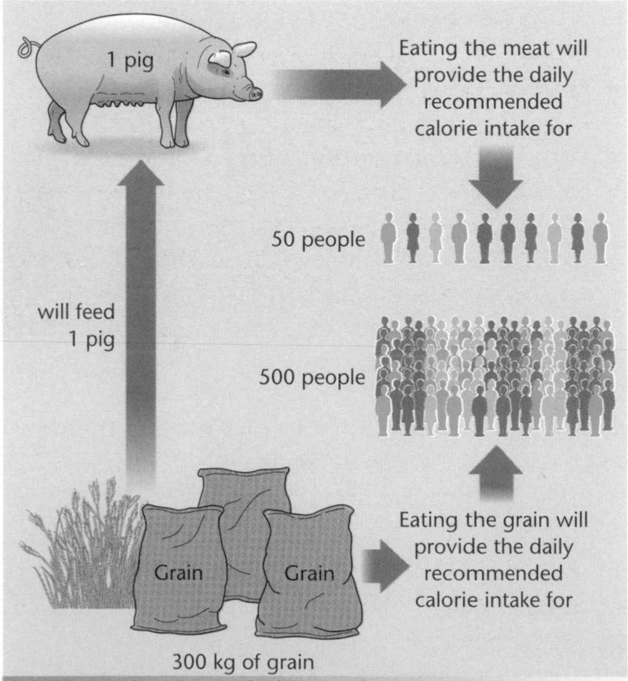

A The implications of China's changing diet

Food supply problems

- Natural disasters, such as floods and typhoons often destroy crops.
- More food is needed to feed the population but grain prices are kept artificially low by government subsidies; so farmers have little **incentive** to grow more grain.
- The Chinese people are eating more meat, poultry and eggs, which need far more land to produce.
- Arable land is being lost to other land uses at a rate of about 500 000 hectares a year.
- Rivers are drying up and the **water table** is dropping in the north of the country as the demand for water increases.

Possible solutions

- A new law states that each province must not reduce the amount of **arable** land it has.
- Create new arable land by terracing hillsides, reclaiming land or converting parks and other open spaces.
- Import large amounts of grain.
- Improve the farming methods and seeds used to increase yields.
- Divert water from the wetter south to the north for irrigation.
- Impose heavy taxes for converting cropland to non-farming uses.

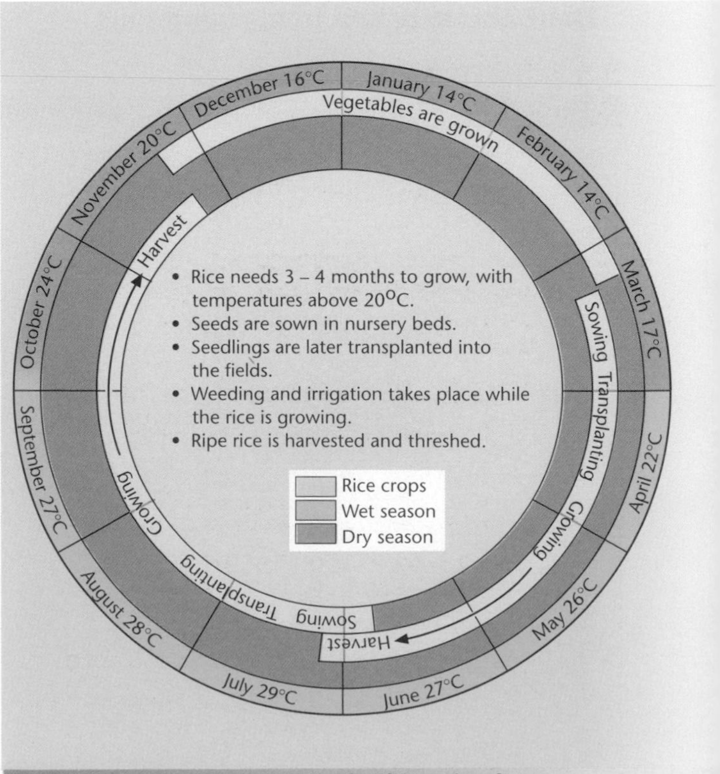

B The farming year on a south China rice farm

C Arable land is being lost at a worrying rate

The old and the new

China has reformed most sections of its economy, and farming is no exception.

The strict communist system has given way to more of a **market economy**, as shown in the boxes below (see also pages 22 and 23).

COMMUNES – THE OLD SYSTEM

- 1 commune = about 2000 households
- Each village (about 200 households) is set a **quota** of how much they have to produce.
- Each family has a small plot of land for their own use.
- Prices are kept low by government subsidies.
- Profits are shared by everyone in the village.
- This system improved production but the ideal crops were often not grown and there was little incentive to produce more.

HOUSEHOLD RESPONSIBILITY – THE NEW SYSTEM

- Individual households are given contracts to lease farmland.
- **Quotas** are set for each piece of land.
- Surpluses are sold by the family.
- Successful groups take up more contracts and can form their own businesses.
- Productivity and profits have increased, but so have prices as subsidies are reduced.
- There has been increased use of fertilisers and a big rise in rural unemployment.

ACTIVITIES

1 Make a list of factors that might increase the chances of a famine in China in the future.

2 a) Write a list of suggestions from a village leader to the government, that might prevent a famine from happening in the future.
b) Look at the possible solutions listed in the text. Suggest some of the drawbacks for each one.

3 a) How many rice crops are grown on the South China farm in diagram **B**?
b) What factors make this possible?
c) Vegetables fetch five times the price of rice. How might this lead to changes on the farm under the new system of household responsibility?

4 Imagine that you are a farmer under the new household responsibility scheme. You have been asked to write a report for the local party official about how the system is working. Outline the ways in which the new system may have brought improvements and problems.

5 Why might other countries be worried if China has problems feeding its population?

6 a) Where will most of the arable land be found, and why is that also the best land for other uses?
b) What problems and conflicts may occur as a result of this?

The Three Gorges Scheme

▶ Why is energy production from this scheme so important to China?
▶ Why is there so much controversy about the scheme?

Rising energy demand

The demand for energy in China is growing rapidly. The population is growing and becoming more affluent. Industries use 65% of China's electricity but frequently operate below capacity due to a shortage of power. Diagram A shows how energy use in China has grown. The figures are forecast to double by 2005, and again by 2020.

Year	1950	1960	1970	1980	1990	1994
Electricity consumption	5	30	76	301	535	780

A Increasing energy use in China (kilowatt hours per person)

Sources of energy

The burning of coal in China causes huge amounts of pollution and results in health problems and damage to the environment (page 30). Coal is also a non-renewable fuel, which will run out at some time, so China is looking at other sources of energy for the future. Is hydro-electric power (HEP) a suitable alternative?

Source of energy	Coal	Oil	Natural gas	Hydro-power
% of total used	75	17.5	1.5	6

B Energy consumption in China, 1996

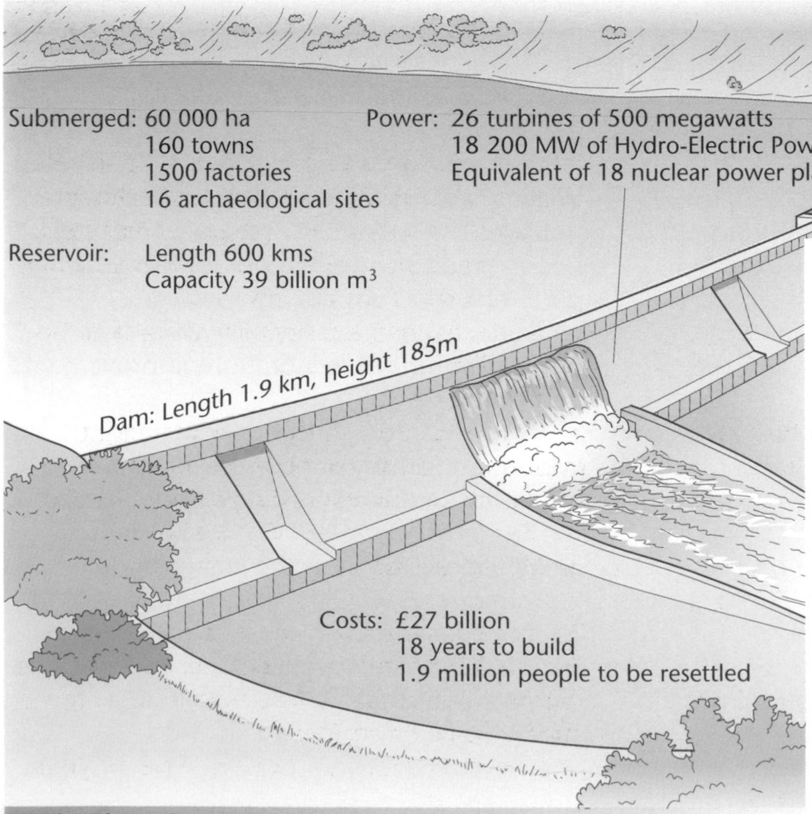

C The Three Gorges Dam: costs and benefits

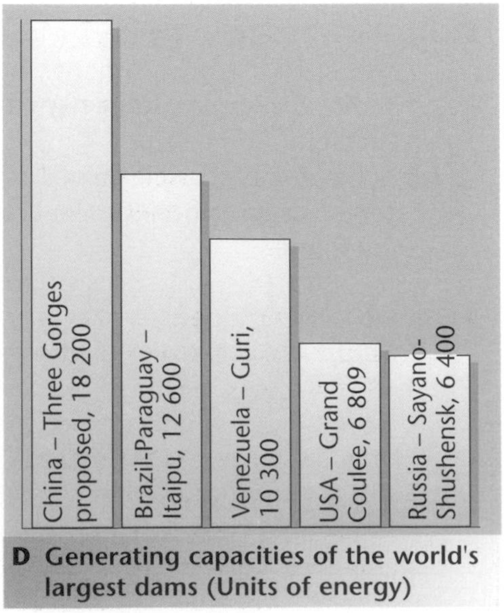

D Generating capacities of the world's largest dams (Units of energy)

A variety of opinions

The Three Gorges Scheme at Sandouping on the Yangtze River is the most ambitious engineering project in China since the building of the Great Wall. There has, however, been strong debate about this Scheme both inside and outside China.

E Yangtze River Gorge

ACTIVITIES

1 a) Describe the change in electricity consumption figures in China from 1950 to 1994.

b) Why is the Chinese use of electricity per person rising so rapidly?

2 a) What is the main source of energy in China?

b) In what ways is HEP thought to be a better source of energy for China than coal?

3 a) What is a gorge?

b) Why is a gorge a good site for building a dam across a river?

4 a) Why might the Three Gorges project be called a multi-purpose scheme?

b) Conduct a class debate or role-play about whether the scheme should go ahead or not. You can propose a motion to debate or share out roles, such as those shown above. You may include more characters, such as a local farmer, local factory owner, government spokesperson, an archaeologist, a resident of an area to be flooded, and so on.

5 In what ways do you think people might respond differently in your country if 1.9 million of them were resettled for a scheme like the Three Gorges? Why would there be such differences?

6 Research other dam schemes around the world that caused major debate. You may use the Internet to gather information from the International Rivers Network http://www.irn.org/index.html. Present your findings to the class.

China's boom industry: tourism

▶ **What have been the benefits and problems of China's rapidly growing tourist industry?**

Advantages of tourism

Tourism has been increasing in China since 1978, when the country opened its frontiers to the outside world. Since then the tourist industry has grown rapidly as a result of improvements in transport and the increased number of hotels. The benefits have been an increase in foreign currency flowing into China and in employment, for example, in the hotel and travel industries.

A typical holiday package for many visitors involves a two-week, four-centre holiday. Visitors fly between cities where they stay (map **B**), and from where they travel to famous historical or scenic sites.

	1980	1985	1990	1996
Total number of international tourists (10 000 persons)	570.3	1783.3	2746.2	5112.8
Foreigners	52.9	137.1	174.7	674.4
Overseas Chinese	3.4	8.5	9.1	15.5
Visitors from Hong Kong, Macao and Taiwan	513.9	1637.8	2562.3	4422.9
Total Foreign Exchange earnings from international tourism (USD 100 million)	6.2	12.5	22.2	102.0

A Growth of tourism in China

		(10 000 persons)	
Country	**1990**	**1994**	**1996**
Total	174.7	518.2	674.4
Japan	46.3	114.1	154.9
Korea	5.5	34.0	69.4
USA	23.2	47.0	57.6
Russia	11.0	74.3	55.6
UK	7.9	16.7	20.5
Thailand	6.8	16.4	19.3
Australia	5.0	11.0	13.3
France	5.1	11.2	12.3
Switzerland	1.2	2.8	3.3
New Zealand	1.0	2.0	3.0

The data of Russia in 1990 and 1994 refer to the former USSR.

C Where the visitors to China come from

Some disadvantages

The increase in tourism has created problems at some of these sites.

Overcrowding

Visits are concentrated because the climate in many areas of China creates a high season in summer (see pages 8 and 9).

Tourist wear and tear

Large numbers of visitors create a physical impact on the features they come to see. The steps on the Great Wall, for example, are well worn. Visitors are reminded not to carve on the bricks, but there is often vandalism.

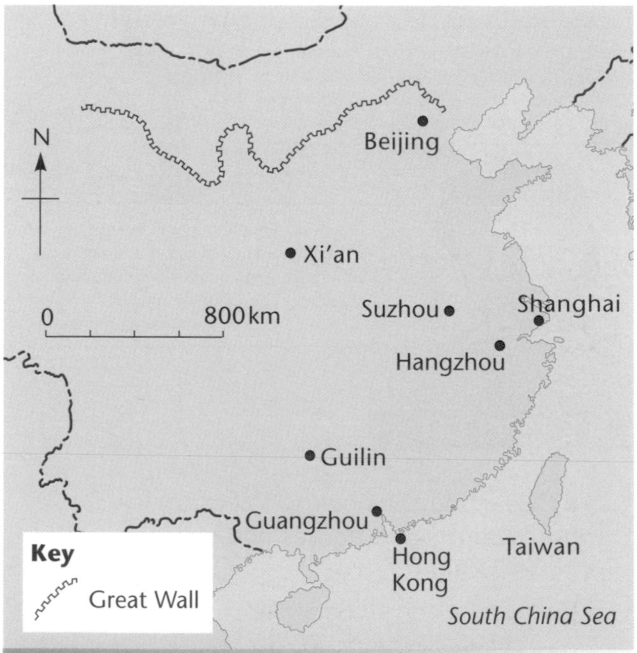

B Main cities where foreign visitors stay

D Tourists on the Great Wall of China

Restoration and development

Restoration of the sites is often needed, for example, an appeal fund has been launched to restore parts of the Great Wall. More visitor centres are needed to explain the history of the sites.

Traffic congestion

Increased tourism has created atmospheric pollution and heavy traffic congestion.

E Tourists on the River Li, Guilin

Tourist honeypot

Guilin is one of China's main tourist honeypots. It is located in Guanxi province. Visitors are attracted to the Li River which is surrounded by a unique form of **Karst** scenery. Tourism has transformed the city. Between 1996 and 1998 a new airport and railway station were opened to cope with the increased number of visitors. Several major new roads were also built.

Number of domestic tourists:	8.4 million
Number of foreign tourists:	450 213
Income from domestic tourists:	14.4 million yuan
Income from foreign tourists	
Sale of products:	2.6 million yuan.
Sale of services:	9.2 million yuan
Increase in number of tourists compared with 1990	
Domestic tourists	11 per cent
Foreign tourists	20 per cent
(Because of the Asia economic crisis, the number of foreign tourists visiting Guilin from January to July 1998 reduced by one third.)	

F Tourism in Guilin: facts and figures for 1997

Month	Jan	Feb	Mar	Apr	May	Jun	Jul	Aug	Sep	Oct	Nov	Dec
Percentage of hotel rooms occupied	29	42	60	61	70	62	63	71	60	78	60	36

G Occupancy rate in Guilin's hotels, 1997

ACTIVITIES

1 Study table **A**. Suggest three reasons to explain why there was an increase in foreign visitors to China between 1980 and 1996.

2 Study table **C**.
a) Describe the pattern of visitors to China from different countries.
b) Suggest reasons for the pattern you have described.

3 Study table **G**.
a) Describe the monthly variations in the occupancy rate in Guilin's hotels during 1997.
b) Suggest the factors that might affect this pattern of occupancy.
c) How might the variation in occupancy during the year affect Guilin's local economy?

4 Write a short account of the likely views of each of the following about the growth of tourism in China:
- a young unemployed person living in Guilin;
- a young conservationist living near the Great Wall;
- a retired school teacher living in Beijing.

5 Refer again to diagram **C** on page 32. Now write an account of your views on the development of tourism in China under the following headings:
- economic losses and gains;
- environmental losses and gains;
- social losses and gains.

6 Compare and contrast the tourist industries of China and another country you have studied, under the following headings:
- where overseas tourists come from;
- the main tourist centres;
- benefits to the economy;
- impact on the environment and society.

Changing jobs

- ▶ What is employment structure?
- ▶ How and why is the employment structure in China changing?

Different types of jobs

There are many different kinds of jobs and people often put them into small groups of similar types to make it easier to look for patterns of employment. Putting jobs into groups, or classifying them, can be done in a number of different ways. One classification divides them into primary, secondary or tertiary employment.

- The *primary sector* includes all jobs involved with obtaining **raw materials**, such as food, minerals and timber. Examples of such jobs include fishing and forestry.
- The *secondary sector* contains all those jobs that turn raw materials into something more useful, such as food processing, steel making, engineering or carpentry.
- The *tertiary sector* is made up of jobs that do not produce anything, but they provide a service, such as shopkeepers, police, drivers or nurses.

(Some people add a separate *quaternary sector* which consists of economic activities concerned with getting or giving information, such as research, finance, law, education and the media.)

Country	Primary % (Farming)	Secondary % (Industry)	Tertiary % (Services)	GNP per person (US$)
China, 1952	84	7	9	50 (est)
China, 1996	73	14	13	620
India, 1996	62	11	27	340
Italy, 1996	9	32	59	19 020
Japan, 1996	6	34	60	39 640

Source: United Nations

A Variations in jobs and wealth

Employment structure

The percentage of jobs in each sector is called the employment structure. It will vary between different countries and will change over time (table **A**). In the economically developing countries of the world, the number of jobs in agriculture and manufacturing declined as services increased. In China, even though there have also been changes in the figures, there are still estimated to be more than half a billion people working in agriculture.

Diagram **B** is a triangular graph and this can be used as a way of showing the employment structure of places.

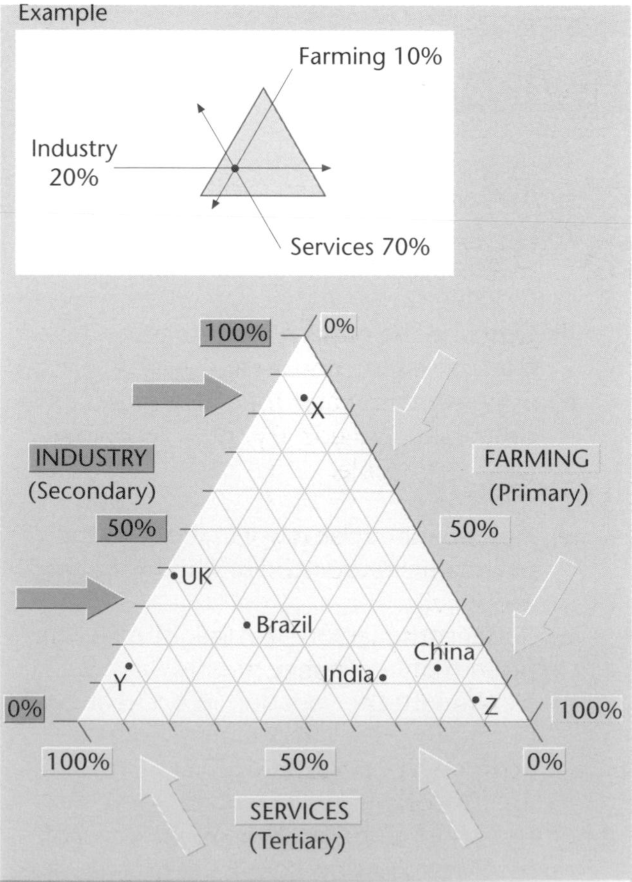

B Triangular graph showing employment structures, 1996

Changes to the employment structure of countries

You may notice a pattern in table **A**. The richer countries (see GNP per person in the last column) have very few people working in the primary sector and have most people working in the tertiary sector. As farming becomes more efficient, the number of labourers employed is reduced. Machines are introduced to replace workers. More money is available for investment into manufacturing industry and people have more time and money to spend on services, such as education, recreation and entertainment.

Increased use of agricultural machinery in China (kilowatts per hectare of cultivated land)		
1985	**1990**	**1995**
2.1	3.0	3.8

C More machines, fewer jobs

Tertiary growth

As more people pour into the cities, the Chinese government expects the tertiary sector to expand to 38% of total employment by 2010. Amongst the potential new growth sectors are tourism, real estate, chain stores, information services, advertising, entertainment, banking and insurance.

Primary workers – most Chinese people in the past and in the rural areas today

Secondary worker – most Chinese workers in the towns and cities today

Tertiary worker – most Chinese workers in the whole country in the future?

D The changing nature of employment in China

ACTIVITIES

1 a) Give two extra examples of jobs in each of the primary, secondary and tertiary sectors.
b) In what other ways do you think jobs could be classified? Try to list as many ways as possible.

2 a) Use the triangular graph to calculate the employment structure of the UK and Brazil.
b) Does letter X, Y or Z on the graph show the employment structure figures for China in 1952?

3 a) How has the employment structure in China changed since 1952?
b) Why do you think these changes occurred?

4 a) What factors do you think will affect China's employment structure in the future?
b) Why do you think China wants to develop the secondary and tertiary sectors of their economy?

5 a) Why are so many Chinese people still employed in agriculture?
b) What might the effects be if many of these jobs are lost as agriculture becomes more efficient? (Pages 16 and 17 (migration) may help you.)

6 The Chinese government figures for employment are: primary 51%, secondary 23% and tertiary 26%. Why do you think their figures are so different from those of organisations such as the United Nations?

China's changing rural economy

▶ **What has been the impact of the rapid growth of village and township enterprises in China's rural areas?**

China has a rural population of 900 million, more than three and a half times the population of the United States. Approximately one third of the people living in rural China are **underemployed**, which explains why 100 million migrate into China's cities for work.

Since the late 1970s there has been a move towards a market economy in the rural areas to try to increase employment. Many small enterprises have been set up, either owned collectively by people in villages or small towns, or run privately.

Some enterprises are small, for example, kerbside selling or workshops manufacturing farm tools and equipment. Others are larger non-agricultural enterprises that obtained loans for factories to process local raw materials or manufacture products. These rural enterprises have brought benefits but also created problems within China's rural areas.

A

Change comes to the village of Nangaoying

Looking out of the window of his new home, He Shengguo sees pleasant open spaces. His family is among the first in Nangaoying, a village near the city of Shijiazhuang in Hebei Province, to move into the new apartment building. More than a dozen 6-storey buildings stand in the new residential area, with gardens, a playground and satellite antennas. It is a sharp contrast to the old village, a scattering of tattered low houses.

Although their status as farmers remain unchanged and each is still given land, they no longer earn most of their living by toiling in the fields all year long. In fact, most of the villagers are now factory workers. These people lived in poverty until ten years ago. Grain used to be the only source of income. The number of young people migrating from the village to large cities such as Beijing has now reduced dramatically.

He Shengguo is the secretary of the village Party Committee. It was he who led the villagers to a better life by launching village enterprises, starting with a small commercial foundry. Huashu Pharmaceutical Factory, the largest local business and the pride of the village, is the largest Terramycin producer in the country and exports 70% of its production overseas.

Most enterprises in Nangaoying are owned and run by the villagers and every village has its own production and distribution system, forming a "village economy" model. The village enterprises have given the people a much better life. For example, Nangaoying now has its own school, hospital, home for the elderly and other public service facilities. Villagers' income is composed of their salary from the village enterprises, distribution of profits from the village and the sale of grain.

It's hard to change the lifestyle and thinking of Nangaoying's farmers, whether they earn their living from the land or by other means. Although agriculture contributes only a small proportion of income, no household seems willing to give up its land. Also, most villagers were slow to accept the apartment buildings. Although subsidies are offered to enhance agricultural production, grain yields remain at medium levels. This makes He Shengguo feel uneasy. He claims that industrial development has been emphasised to the loss of agriculture in recent years.

Eventually, the city of Shijiazhuang will swallow up Nangaoying. A newly built ring road already encloses quite a large part of the village's farmland.

China Today, February 1999

Some problems created by the village and township enterprises

- Loss of cultivated land for food supply.
- Loss of land plus increasing mechanisation means that fewer people are needed in farming.
- In the more remote areas there are high transport costs and difficulties in making market contacts.
- Absence of planning in many areas.
- Lack of effective financial management and corruption in some areas.
- Poor working conditions and high accident rates in some places.
- Destruction of the environment, for example, brick-making destroys the land and lime-making reduces the forest cover.

B The location of Nangaoying

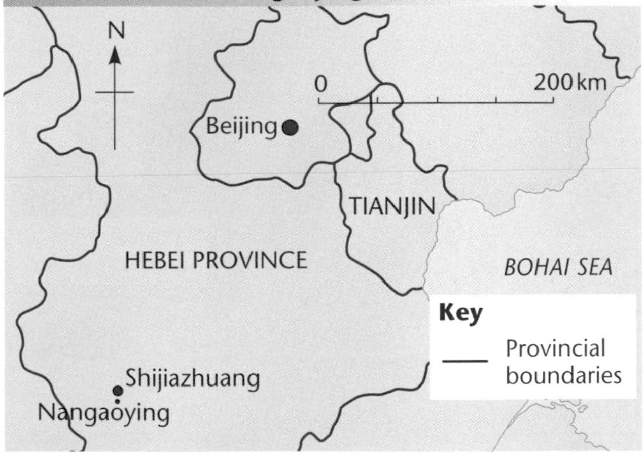

Year	Population (millions)
1984	76
1990	94
1998	135

C Employment in China's village and township enterprises

Sector	% contribution
Electronic communications equipment	17
Machinery	26
Raw coal and cement	40
Food and Beverages	43
Clothing	80

D Contribution of income to China's economy from village and township enterprises

E Making shoes in a township enterprise

ACTIVITIES

1 Explain what is meant by the terms 'market economy' and 'an underemployed workforce.'

2 Using map **B** and an atlas describe the location of Nangaoying in China.

3 Study extract **A** and map **B**. Explain why Nangaoying's location might be an advantage for the development of the village's economy.

4 Read the information in extract **A**. Summarise the benefits of village enterprises to Nangaoying's residents. Suggest two disadvantages.

5 Why is the reduction of underemployment in rural areas so important politically to the Chinese government? Use information from extract **B** on page 56 to help you with your answer.

6 Study the data in tables **C** and **D**. Write a short paragraph about village and township enterprises in China. Include information on how these businesses have grown, and which types of rural business contribute most to the economy.

7 Name a rural area in another country you have studied which experiences underemployment. Explain the steps that were taken to reduce this underemployment.

Made in China

- ▶ **Why does a major American company locate a factory in China?**
- ▶ **What are the benefits for all those concerned?**

The background

Black and Decker is a long established, trans-national American company that manufactures a variety of power tools. In the early 1990s the company lost 25% of its sales in Europe to cheaper, poorer quality, imports from China. Black and Decker decided to form a **joint venture company** with a Chinese firm (Chiaphua), in order to start **manufacturing** in China themselves. This enabled Black and Decker to set up in China quickly, using Chiaphua's existing staff, contacts and expertise, without the difficulties of starting fresh. Black and Decker Chiaphua International Limited (BDCI) began operation in 1996 at a factory in Shajing. Production and sales from the factory in China doubled in the first two years and are continuing to grow impressively.

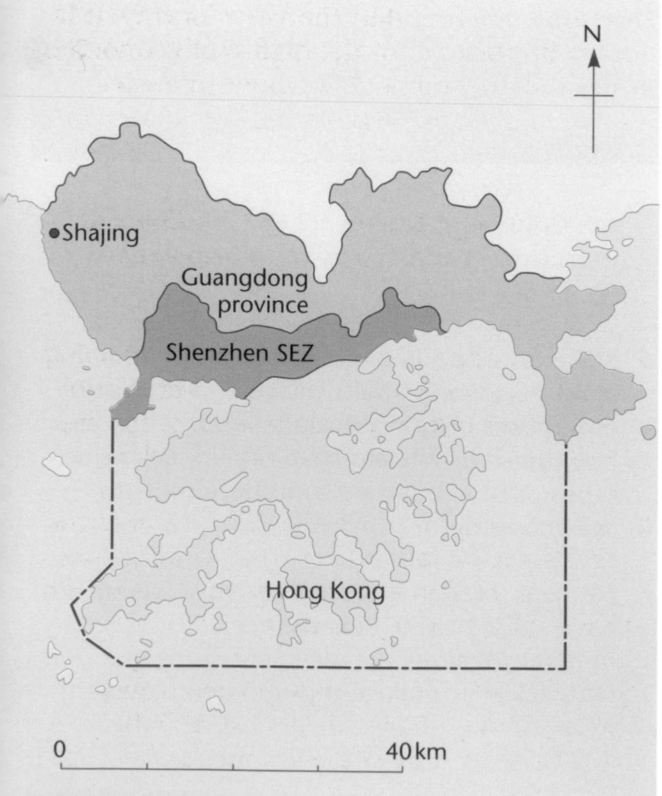

B Location of Shajing

The manufacturing system

The **manufacturing** system consists of inputs, processes and outputs. For BDCI the inputs come from a variety of locations worldwide. However, 60% or more of the materials used are from China, since this avoids having to pay European Union import duties.

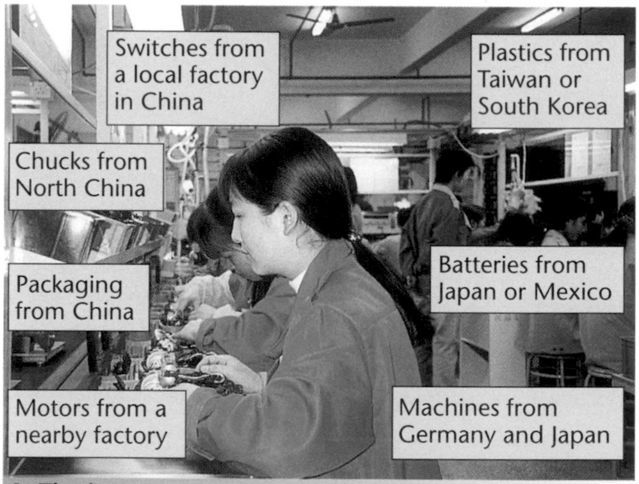

A The inputs – an example of globalisation

C Employers and employees are winners

Advantages for BDCI

- Workers are paid US$12 a week (compared to over $200 a week in USA).
- Other overheads and infrastructure costs are low.
- All imports and exports are duty free.
- Sample products can be produced quickly and at 20% of the cost in Europe.

Advantages for the workers

- Wages are three times what workers would get at home in north China.
- Workers get dormitory accommodation, canteen, sports, health and social facilities provided free.
- Within three years workers can save enough money to buy a house or shop back home.

The processes
The factory is divided into about 40 manufacturing cells where assembly of the different products is carried out, followed by quality control and distribution. The company also has design facilities and a reliability test centre.

The outputs
BDCI produce a range of cordless power tools, mainly drills and screwdrivers. These are sold all over the world, but mainly in the USA and Europe.

The workforce
The factory employs 2000 workers, mostly aged around 18 – 20 and 85% of them female. The workers are brought in from the north of China because local people have become too well off to work for the wages offered (see pages 16 and 17). Workers usually choose to work around 60 hours a week, rather than the standard 44 hours, to earn as much money as possible. The management is made up mostly of Hong Kong Chinese or 'westerners' and the Head Office of the company is still located in Hong Kong. Although Hong Kong costs are ten times as high, the necessary skills and **infrastructure** are still not thought to be well enough developed to locate fully in China.

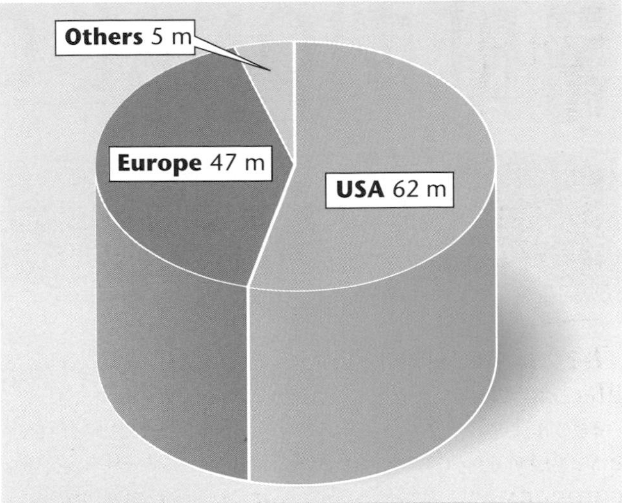

D 1998 Black and Decker sales profile, $millions

The competition
The company has developed a fully integrated plant at Shajing in order to reduce production costs even further. The factory is not only competing with rival companies, but also with other Black and Decker plants around the world. Output from Shajing is growing at a rate of 50% a year at present, and it has taken over work from factories in the UK and North America. The cost advantages make this site an ideal place for manufacturing industry. Many other foreign companies such as Sanyo and Panasonic are found in the same locality. It is almost impossible for the high-cost economies of the west to compete in labour-intensive industries such as this.

ACTIVITIES

1 a) Make a list of reasons why Black and Decker decided to open a factory in China.
b) Why did they form a joint venture company with a Chinese firm?

2 a) On a world outline map, mark China and the location of the BDCI company. Draw labelled arrows to show the sources of the factory's inputs.
b) Add other labels to show the location of head office, sources of the workforce, and the main markets for the products.
c) Write a short summary to explain what makes Shajing a particularly suitable location for the factory.

3 List **C** shows the advantages for BDCI and for the workers of having the factory here. Write down some of the advantages for China of having such companies in their country.

4 Imagine that you are a BDCI factory worker from the north of the country who is deciding whether to go home for good. Make a list of the advantages and disadvantages of staying. How would you make your final decision?

5 Who do you think benefits the most from the factory being located in China? Give reasons for your answer and compare your views with those of others in your class.

6 How do you think the advantages of this location may change in the future? What will the effects be of the changes that you predict?

5 REGIONAL CONTRASTS

A country with regional inequalities

- How do levels of development vary within China?
- What are the main reasons for the regional differences in development?

Like many countries, China has marked contrasts in the levels of development between its regions. One way to help explain differences in development between regions is to use the idea of core and periphery.

A A village in Shaanxi Province

Core regions are those where there is a great deal of economic activity, such as industry and finance; most of a country's wealth is concentrated here. In China, the core regions are on the coast in provinces such as Guangdong.

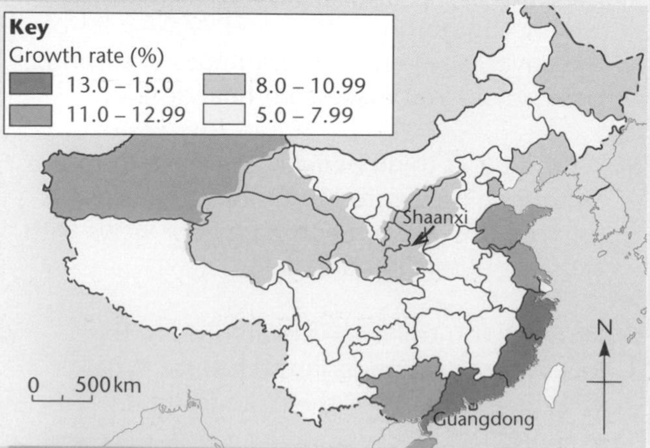

C Average annual growth of GNP, 1985 – 97

Away from the cores there are less wealthy areas: the periphery. Here there is less economic activity and standards of living are lower. In China the periphery is in the centre and west of the country, in provinces such as Shaanxi.

As in other countries, China's core regions have grown at the expense of the periphery. For example, many of the more enterprising workers have left the interior for the coastal areas. This has created a number of social difficulties within the country. Some people believe that if the regional inequalities within China become greater, the country's political stability might be threatened.

B Guangzhou, Guangdong Province

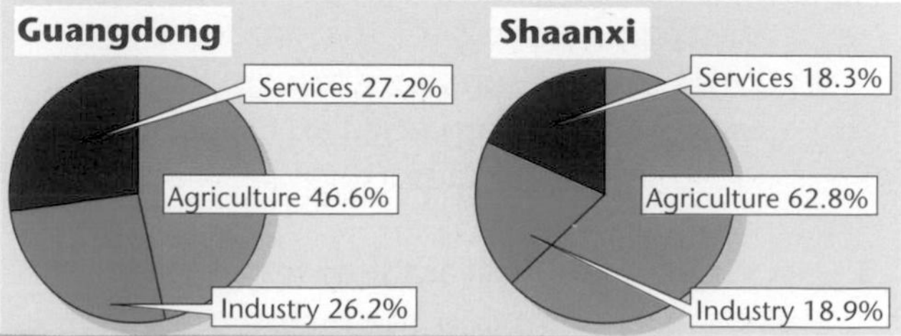

D Types of employment

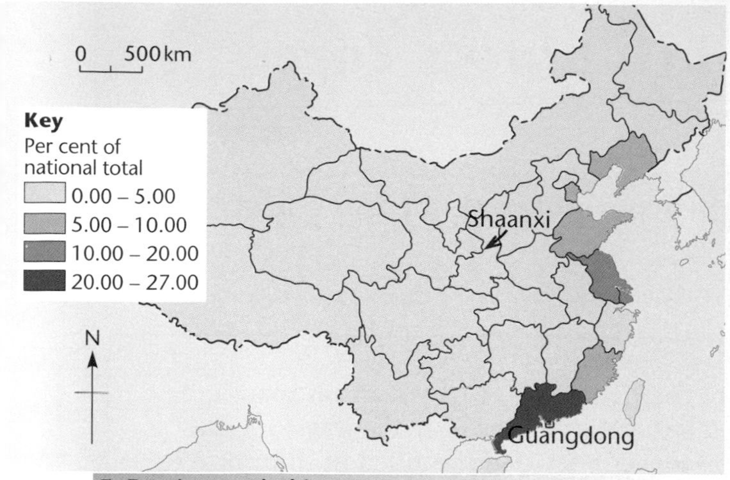

E Foreign capital investment, 1997

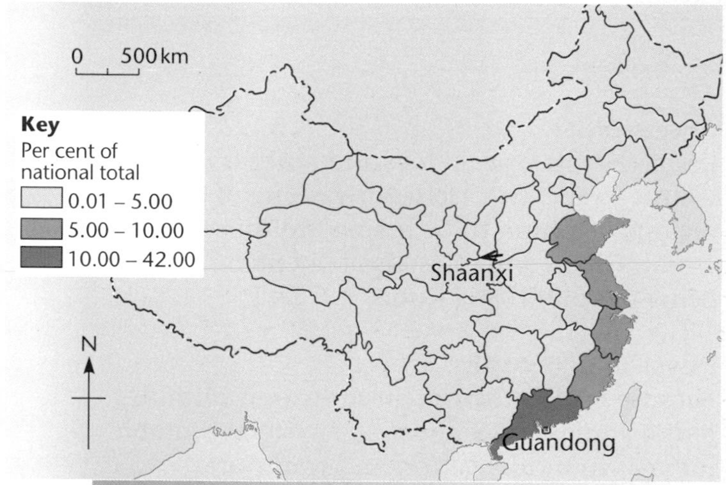

F Exports from China's provinces, 1997

	Guangdong	Shaanxi
Area (km^2)	178 000	205 500
Population 1992 (m)	65.25	34.05
% urban 1991	29.79	24.6

G Key facts

	Guangdong	Shaanxi
Average annual wage (Rmb)	4 027	2434
For agricultural workers	2 730	2095
For industrial workers	4 178	2441

H Average annual wage, 1992

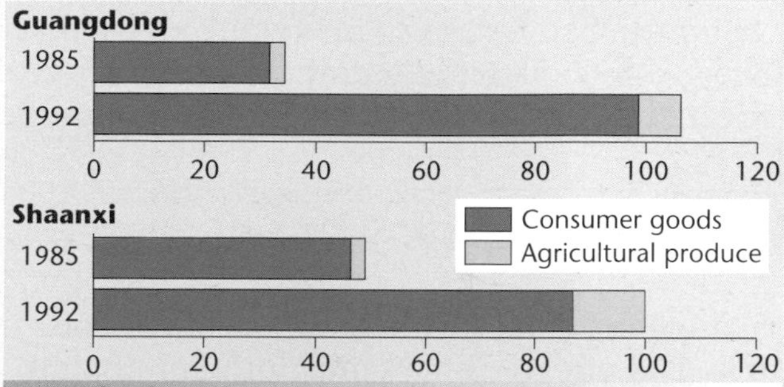

I Total value of retail sales

Ownership of mobile phones	Guangdong	Shaanxi
	82 987	1 790

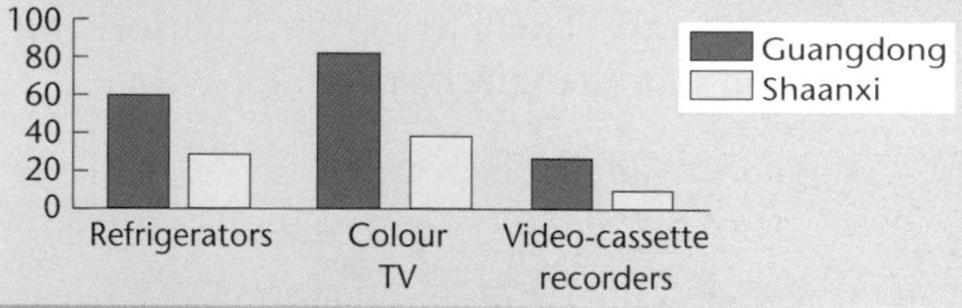

J Ownership of consumer goods per 100 households

ACTIVITIES

1 From the information on pages 34 and 35, and on these two pages, list the various ways in which development can be defined.

2 a) Draw labelled sketches of photographs **A** and **B** to illustrate the differences in development between Guangdong and Shaanxi Provinces.

b) Using information from tables **H**, **I** and **J**, explain why people from the village shown in photograph **A** might improve their living standards by moving from Shaanxi Province to Guangzhou in Guangdong Province.

3 Using the information on maps **C**, **E** and **F**, and the map of China's provinces on Page 5:

a) name three provinces in China's core, other than Guangdong.

b) Name three provinces in China's periphery, other than Shaanxi.

4 Draw a larger version of the table below. Use the information on these two pages and ideas from your previous studies in this book to complete your table.

	Factors affecting China's regional development	Ways in which the factor affects development
1		
2		
3		
4		

5 Explain why differences in wealth within China could cause the country's political stability to be threatened.

Guangdong Province in China's core

- **Why is Guangdong one of the most prosperous parts of the country?**
- **How might it develop in the future?**

> In my travels around China's southern provinces of Guangdong, I discovered that roads are being built so fast, in so many directions, that no maps are accurate. To make way for cities erected in a matter of months, mountains are being moved, rice paddies filled in, forests cleared … It is a sight the likes of which few people alive today have seen.

Paul Theroux, *Going to See the Dragon*

Guangdong is located in China's coastal core area. It is one of China's most prosperous and heavily populated provinces. Its population increased from 54 million in 1986 to 68 million in 1995. The maps on pages 48 and 49 illustrate the importance of Guangdong in China's economy. There are several reasons for Guangdong's amazing economic growth:

A Guangdong within China's core

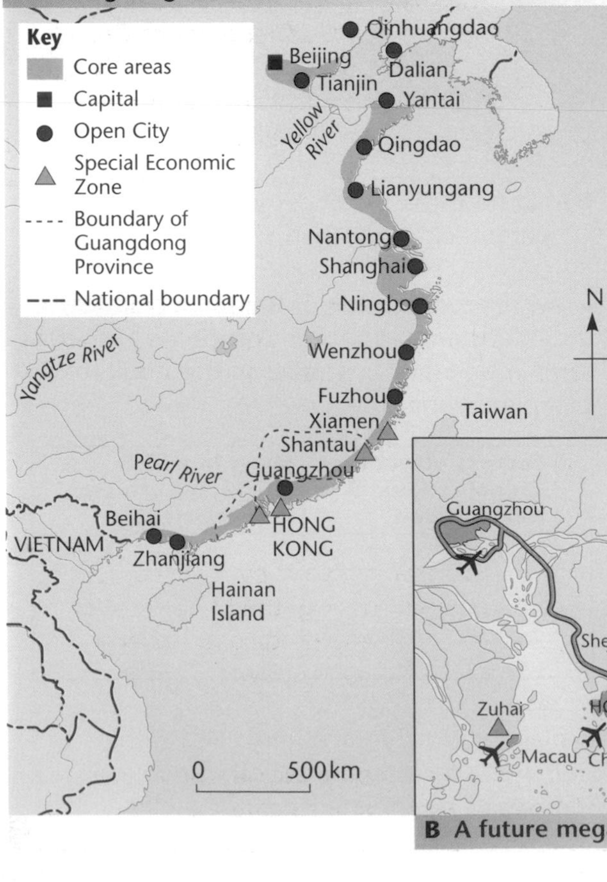

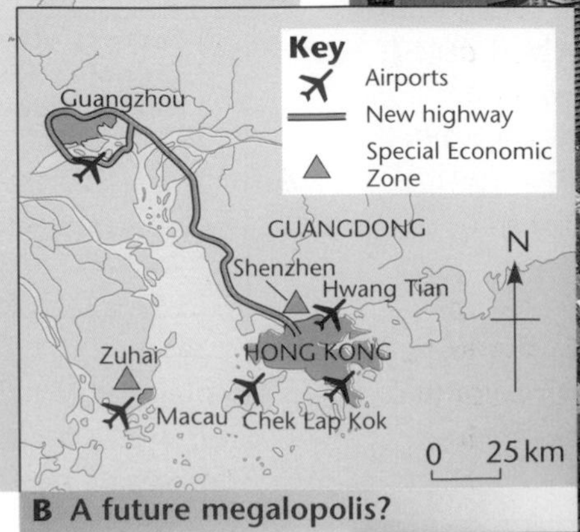

B A future megalopolis?

Accessibility

Because of its coastal location and easy access via the Pearl River Delta, it was one of the first regions of China to be opened to the outside world. Guangdong has also benefited from being close to Hong Kong.

Physical geography

Because of its **subtropical monsoon climate**, fertile alluvial soils and water systems suitable for year-round irrigation and transportation, it is a major agricultural region (see pages 6 – 9).

Political and economic factors

Since 1979 the province has benefited from the Chinese government's decisions to encourage trade and investment in some parts of the country's core area.

C Central Shenzhen

Because of its prosperity Guangdong has become a magnet for China's migrant population. Pages 16 and 17 explain the advantages and disadvantages of this migration.

In 1979, the Chinese government created four small areas along its coast as Special Economic Zones (SEZs). Since 1984, 288 'open cities' have been established, mainly along the coast. Firms locating here are given cost and tax incentives. Guangdong Province has three SEZs and one open city. These areas are open to the rest of the world for trade and investment.

Shenzhen SEZ, in Guangdong, on the border of the Hong Kong Special Administrative Region, is 327 km^2 in size. In 1979 it was a small market town of 30 000 people and had 1 500 factories. In 1995 its population was 1.4 million, with 25 000 factories.

Most of the factories are owned by Hong Kong businesses (see pages 46 and 47). The owners do not pay customs duties on goods. Mainland Chinese people are employed in jobs needing large amounts of labour. Highly skilled work is still done in Hong Kong.

Average costs (1997)	Shenzhen Special Economic Zone	Hong Kong Special Administrative Region
Monthly wages (manufacturing industry)	US$150	US$1 420
Factory premises selling price/m^2	US$200	US$3 878
Office premises monthly rental/m^2	US$10	US$73
High rise flats (selling price/m^2)	US$900	US$11 368
Cost of electricity (per kwh)	US$0.07	US$0.11
Number of foreign firms	14 500	4 943

D Shenzhen's economic advantages

"By 2010 Macau, Shenzhen, Zhuhai and Hong Kong will have developed into a southern China 'megalopolis' with a population of 12 million. The development of science and technology based industries and improved transport links will make this one of the most prosperous urban areas in the world.

Many Hong Kong people will live in Shenzhen and travel to work in Hong Kong. Other areas of China's core will become **megalopolises**, for example the area between Beijing and Tianjin."

E A Shenzhen town planner

ACTIVITIES

1 Study map **A**.
  a) How many special economic zones are there?
  b) How many open cities are there?
  c) What do you notice about the location of special economic zones and 'open cities' in China? Suggest reasons for their location.

2 Study table **D**. Calculate the cost of the following:
- buying a factory with 2000 m^2 of floor space in (i) Shenzhen and (ii) Hong Kong
- renting an office with 500 m^2 of floor space in (i) Shenzhen and (ii) Hong Kong;

3 Work in pairs. You are business consultants to a foreign company deciding whether to establish a computer factory in either Shenzhen or Hong Kong. Write an advisory report for the company based on the information on these two pages, and pages 48 and 49.

4 **a)** Explain what is meant by a 'megalopolis'.
  b) Suggest reasons why the Shenzhen town planner believes a megalopolis will develop in the area shown on map **B** by 2010.

5 Write five sentences to explain why the coast of China is the country's core area.

Shaanxi Province in China's periphery

- **Why are there poverty-stricken areas in provinces such as Shaanxi?**
- **How can these levels of poverty be reduced?**

Shaanxi Province, in the middle west of China, is part of the country's periphery. Its provincial capital is Xi'an, the former capital of China. More than 80% of Shaanxi consists of mountains and hills. The climate is continental monsoon. The province's gross national product is approximately one third below the average for the country as a whole. Shaanxi's population of 34 million contains 6% of China's most poverty-stricken rural people. The Ankang region, in the Province's Qinba Mountains, is one of its most deprived areas.

SOME CHARACTERISTICS OF THE ANKANG REGION'S POPULATION

- Half the boys and nearly all the girls do not attend school.
- Illiteracy rates are very high.
- **Infant mortality rates** are between 15 and 20% (more than 50% above the national average).
- Many people have severe vitamin deficiencies.
- Maternal mortality rates are 0.5% (100% above the national average).
- There is a high incidence of tuberculosis.
- Roughly half the children are partly stunted in growth because of malnutrition.
- 90% of the children suffer chronic intestinal worm infection.
- Average annual income is 530 yuan (£37).

Why the region's poverty level is high

- The area is mountainous which means that there is very little agricultural land.
- It is difficult for the population to earn sufficient income from cash crops so there is severe underemployment.
- Unlike some rural areas of China, migration to the cities for work is very restricted.
- The area is isolated and there is a serious shortage of both roads and vehicles.
- The population lacks information about job prospects in other parts of the country.
- Individuals have insufficient knowledge and skills to obtain employment.
- They have no spare income to enable them to leave in search of jobs.

A A village in the Qinba Mountains

B Location map of Shaanxi Province

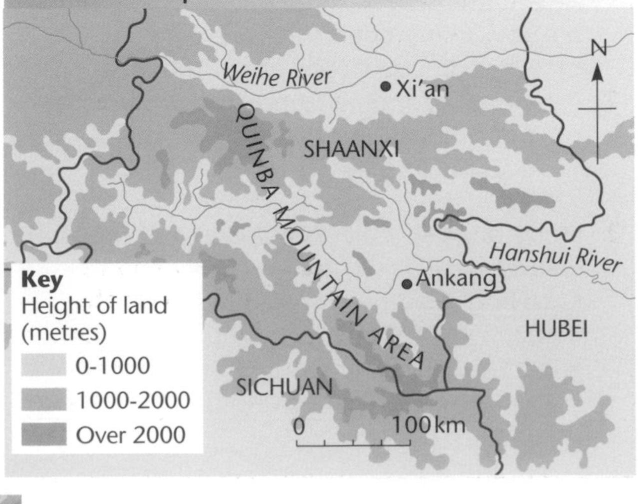

Reducing poverty in Shaanxi

The Chinese government, with the help of funding from the World Bank, has introduced a major welfare project in the Qinba Mountain area. This initiative should benefit the population of the Ankang region.

The project's aims are:

- to reduce poverty by increasing incomes and productivity;
- to improve health and education;
- to reverse the environmental destruction of the upland areas by increasing afforestation;
- to encourage local communities to be involved in decision-making which affects their future.

Other parts of China's periphery with the poorest populations, earning less than 500 yuan per year, include ethnic minority regions in remote **autonomous regions** such as Guangxi, Zhuang, Tibet, Ningxia, Hui and Inner Mongolia. The Chinese government needs to attract more foreign capital to tackle this major problem.

Period	Decrease	Annual average decrease
1978 – 85	250 million to 125 million	17.86 million
1985 – 95	125 million to 65 million	6 million

C Decrease in China's poverty-stricken rural population

Category	% of project funding allocated
Improvements in upland agriculture, e.g. by increasing crop yields on the small amounts of flat land available and creating terraces to improve water and soil conservation	54
Increasing off-farm employment, e.g. by increasing rural labour mobility, providing vocational training, introducing a computerised system for job searching and supporting new rural enterprises such as handicraft industries	30
Improvements in services, e.g. by building health clinics and primary schools, introducing irrigation and rural electrification schemes	11
Developing research and monitoring to ensure that the population in the Ankang region benefits from the Project	4
Providing financial credit for local people to develop co-operative and individual schemes	1

D Main categories of Project funding

ACTIVITIES

1 Define each of the following: maternal mortality rate, afforestation, World Bank and autonomous region.

2 From the figures on page 52, compare average annual incomes in the Ankang region with those in your own country.

3 Using the information on page 52, write an explanation of why the Ankang region's population is poverty-stricken, under the following headings:
- accessibility;
- physical geography;
- economic factors.

4 Work in pairs. Suggest and justify a different balance of funding in the Qinba Mountain Project to that shown in table **D**. Present your views to the whole class.

5 Suggest two reasons why Tibet is even poorer than the Ankang region.

6 Name a poverty-stricken region in another country you have studied. Compare and contrast the region with Ankang under the following headings:
- reasons for low poverty levels;
- methods adopted for reducing poverty.

6 CHINA'S FUTURE

Trade and globalization

▶ How is China's role in the world changing?

It's a small world

Developments such as cable television, the Internet, mobile telephones and cheap air travel seem to have drawn different peoples closer together. European firms frequently use Asian companies to carry out their computer programming. Canadian books may be printed in Hong Kong. Coca Cola and BMW cars can be seen in cities of every continent. This is often a result of the process of **globalization**.

The money pours in

Around 85% of the investment in China is from overseas Chinese who have made their fortunes in places such as Hong Kong, Singapore, Malaysia or Taiwan. In the past these investments were not allowed, but nowadays China has a more open market economy. US trans-national companies, like General Motors and IBM, have contributed more than US$5 billion of the remaining investment.

Year	1981	1986	1991	1996
Primary goods	10.2	11.3	16.1	21.9
Manufactured goods	11.8	19.7	55.7	129.1

A Changing Chinese exports ($US billions)

Changing trade

China is undergoing rapid economic growth and is becoming a major player in the world economic community. In 1978 China was the country ranked 32nd in world trade but by 1996 it had risen to eighth. Many people forecast that its GNP will overtake that of the USA by 2015.

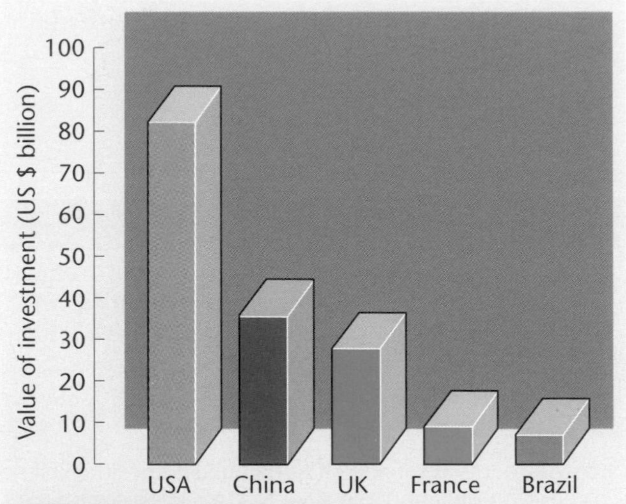

B The top five receivers of foreign investment in 1997

You may not be surprised that clothing and toys are China's top two exports (50% of all toys sold in the world are made in China), but would you know that telecommunications equipment is China's third highest export?

Some of China's advantages

China has the largest home market in the world and one of the fastest growing economies in the world. It also has the most widely spoken first language. It is a member of the Asia-Pacific Economic Co-operation group (APEC), which includes the USA and Japan. APEC accounts for 46% of global trade.

The next 20 years?

The World Bank has made two different predictions for China in the next 20 years. If the present reforms fail then they forecast it will remain a low-income and unequal society, full of possible conflicts. If China succeeds, it will become a middle-income country, with earnings similar to Portugal, South Korea or Argentina. Hundreds of millions of people will be directly affected by the outcome.

C Most widely spoken first languages (% of world population)

%	Language
15.2	Mandarin
5.5	English
4.6	Spanish
3.2	Bengali
3.1	Hindi
2.9	Portuguese
2.9	Russian

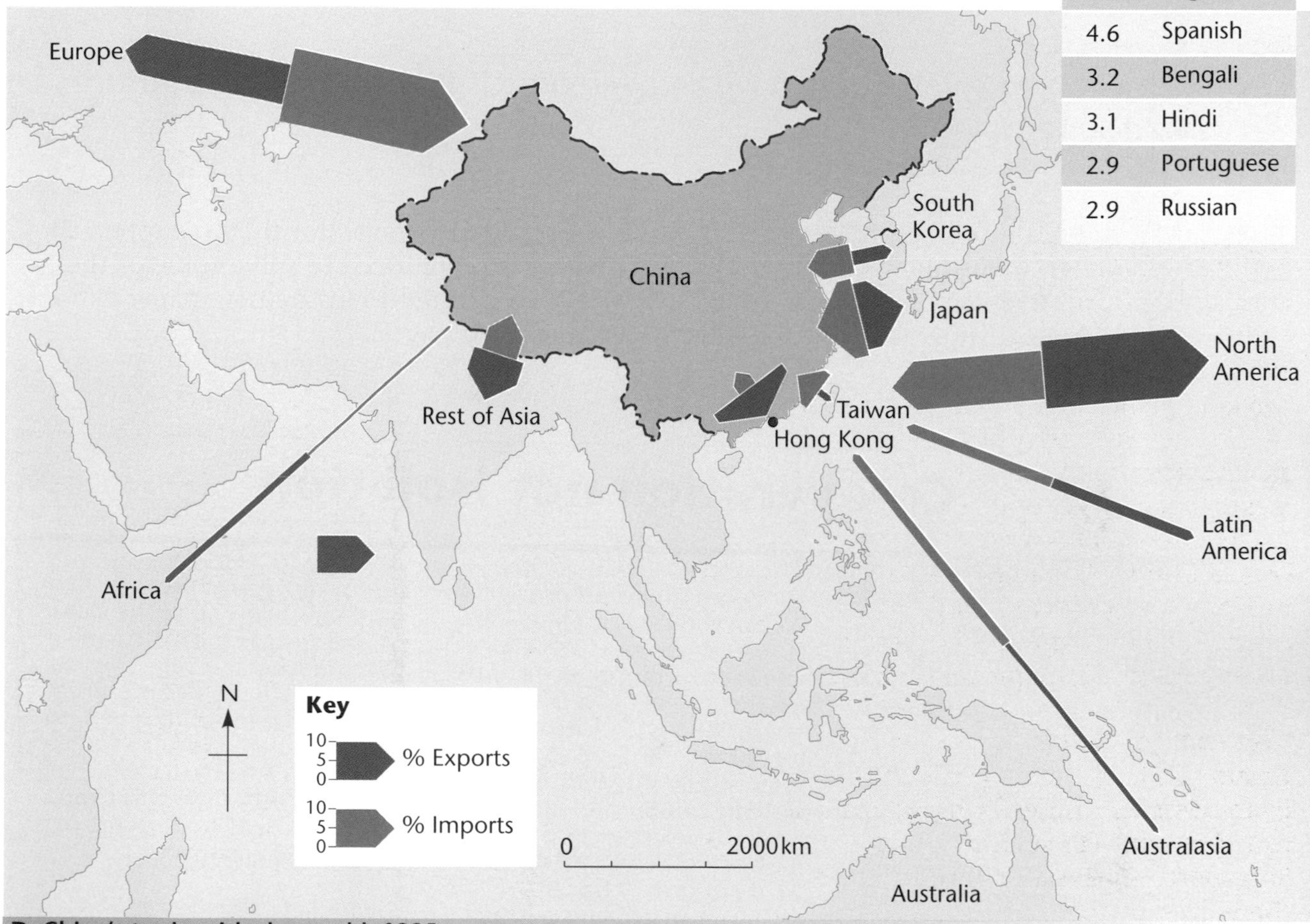

D China's trade with the world, 1995

ACTIVITIES

1 a) Draw a graph to show the changing nature of China's exports, using table **A**.
b) Describe what your graph shows.

2 a) Who are China's main trading partners shown on map **D**?
b) Try to give as many reasons as possible for the pattern of trade shown on the map.

3 In 1996 China had a trade surplus of US$33.7 billion with the USA. What does this mean and why are countries like the USA very concerned?

4 a) What factors, given on this page or elsewhere in the book, suggest that China can become the biggest economy in the world?
b) What advantages and disadvantages might this bring?

5 a) What is meant by globalization? Give examples related to your own life.
b) What changes might have occurred in China to show that globalization is happening?

6 Conduct some research to find out what Chinese products you, your classmates and friends possess. Try to classify them into categories, such as electrical items, clothing, food, and so on. Is there evidence that China is losing its reputation for producing cheap, inferior goods?

China's challenges

▶ What problems will China have to overcome if it is to become a future global superpower?

With its vast natural resources, huge population, foreign investments and new Special Administrative Region of Hong Kong, China could become a superpower in the next few decades. However, for this to happen the government will need to solve some of the problems referred to in the newspaper extracts on these two pages.

A

Co-operation not isolation

In a speech yesterday in Washington, President Clinton said that America must co-operate with China, rather than isolate the country. He went on:

"Already China is one of the fastest growing markets for our goods and services. As we look into the next century, it will support hundreds of thousands of jobs all across our country. But access to China's markets remains restricted for many of our companies and products. We can continue to press China to open its markets as it engages in major economic reform.

Working with China is the best way to advance our interests. By integrating China into the community of nations and the global economy, helping its leadership understand that greater freedom profoundly serves China's interests, and standing up for our principles, we can most effectively serve the cause of democracy and human rights in China.

The Chinese people must have the freedom to speak, to publish, to associate, to worship without fear of reprisal. Only then will China reach its full potential for growth and greatness."

South China Morning Post, 24 June 1998

B

China's rural problems

Protesting workers, rioting peasants and Sunday's bomb explosion in Changsha, the capital of Hunan province, add up to a scary picture of just how bad things are in parts of China. In Mao Zedong's home province, the economic problems are increasing so fast that unrest can easily turn into revolt.

Last year angry workers staged 60 protests outside the provincial party headquarters, so many that the authorities issued an emergency decree on December 29 outlawing further protests. Yet the protests are continuing in this rural province of 60 million. In Changde city, a third of its 10 000 cotton mill factory workers have been laid off without pay, and on Monday, 500 blocked a new highway to press demands for three months' **subsistence wages**. In November, 200 workers from the Laiteer Company blocked traffic in Changsha holding up banners which said: "Not a yuan in six months, we want rice to eat".

Hunan's industrial economy is close to breakdown and the government is bankrupt. From an industrial workforce of four million in **state-owned enterprises** (SOEs), a million have already been fired. The province has 140 SOEs in operation which are losing money, especially in the textile sector. The central government is trying to reduce over-production and return the sector to profitability. Last year it fired 0.5 million textile workers. This year the target is 1.1 million workers. Hunan laid off 21 000 workers last year but the big push was supposed to come this year. "We just can't do it now, it will undermine social stability," a spokesman at the Industrial Management Centre of the Hunan Textile Bureau admitted. "The government is in financial difficulties so it cannot even support the workers already laid off."

South China Morning Post, 23 January 1999

C

Fastest growing economy in the world has fastest growing pollution problem

Just as in the United states in the 1950s, everybody wants a refrigerator in today's emerging consumer society in China. In 1984, only 3 per cent of the households in Beijing owned a fridge. By 1989 this had risen to 60 per cent. The problem is that all these fridges use chlorofluorocarbons as coolant.

Carbon dioxide is the most abundant of greenhouse gases, but pound for pound CFCs are hundreds of times more effective in trapping heat and are extremely persistent.

What remains of China's wildlife is also under threat because of the nation's economic success. The rain forests of the south have all but disappeared, while in the north-west, logging is rapidly reducing swathes of primary conifer forests. Also, climate change might well affect the flora and fauna that inhabit the mountains on the eastern edge of the Tibetan plateau.

Best known and best loved of all the inhabitants of these mountains is the giant panda. Already the panda is one of the world's most seriously endangered animals, and the focus of intense international concern.

Sunday Standard, 11 July 1993

D

China: a country with inequalities

Gogglebox

Villagers in the remote Simao district of Yunnan province watch television for the first time after authorities fixed up a satellite dish.

Life on the footbridge

A migrant couple from Yunnan living on a footbridge overlooking Shanghai's prosperous Bund district.

In 1997, the GNP for Shanghai was 7 954 Rmb per year; for Yunnan it was 1 332 Rmb per year.

ACTIVITIES

1 Study the four newspaper extracts **A**, **B**, **C**, and **D**, and then copy and complete the table below.

Heading of the article	Summary of main problem for China	Reasons why the problem is difficult to solve	Ways in which the problem might be solved

2 Using sources such as newspaper articles and the Internet, write an up-dated account of any of China's problems referred to in the newspaper extracts.

3 Study extract **D**. Describe the feelings of the girl in the photograph who is new to Shanghai.

4 Study extract **A**. Write a response from a Chinese government official to the last paragraph in President Clinton's speech.

5 Describe two other major problems China faces which you have studied in this book.

6 Give three reasons to explain why, although China faces problems, it might still become a world superpower.

Twenty-first century issues

ISSUE 1: can the Chinese government overcome the difficulties caused by the country's ethnic diversity?

About 93% of the population of China is Han Chinese. Approximately 7% of the population consists of 55 different minority nationalities. Examples of the largest minorities are listed in table **A**. Mao Zedong once said:

"China has a vast territory, abundant resources and a large population. Of these three, the Han population possess one, namely, they are many in number; the minority population possesses two, they have vast territories and resources".

Newspaper extract B illustrates how the presence of **ethnic minorities** in China can cause problems for the Government.

A Examples of China's ethnic minorities

Minority	Population	Areas of distribution
Zhuang	13 378 162	Guangxi, Yunnan, Guangdong, Guizhou
Uighurs	6 019 632	Xinjiang, Hunan
Tibetans	3 970 068	Tibet, Sichuan, Qinghai, Gansu, Yunnan
Mongolians	3 411 657	Inner Mongolia, Xinjiang, Liaoning, Jilin, Heilongjiang, Qinghai, Hebei, Yunnan Henan, Gansu

ISSUE 2: will China be able to feed its population?

Two thirds of China is taken up with mountains and deserts. Only 10% of the land is available for cultivation. At its current rate of growth, the Chinese population will reach 1.5 billion by 2015, having trebled in less than ten years. The amount of arable land is reducing and the growth rate in grain production has begun to slow down.

B Glimpse of a troubled land

XINJIANG IN TROUBLE

Bit by bit, a picture is emerging of China's most troubled region, Xinjiang, in the far north-west. For the past year or two, occasional guarded reports in official Chinese newspapers have suggested the existence of separatist movements in the region. Amnesty International has put together the most comprehensive account so far of the persecution of the region's ethnic majority, the Uighurs.

According to Amnesty, Xinjiang is the only region of China where political prisoners are known to have been executed in recent years. The Uighurs are Muslims, so, as in Buddhist Tibet, there is a religious divide between the ethnic locals and the Han Chinese. Many Chinese have migrated to Xinjiang, as they have to Tibet. The Uighurs fear that their culture is being destroyed, and that they will eventually become a minority in their own region. Culture and religion foster the Uighurs' longings for independence. Xinjiang is mostly a desert three times the size of France, but under the ground are oil and other minerals, prizes that drew the Chinese – and keep them there.

The Economist, May 1999

ISSUE 3: can the Chinese government convince western countries that it has an improving human rights record?

Many people in western countries feel that China has a poor record on human rights. They point out the events in Tiananmen Square in Beijing on the night of 4 June 1989 when the Chinese Government ordered its army to fire on protesting students, which resulted in large numbers of deaths. But many Chinese feel that the west has failed to acknowledge what they believe to be their government's improving record on **human rights.**

This is an important issue because the USA in particular wishes to see this improvement before giving China any more concessions for trading with western countries.

ISSUE 4: can the country reduce the inequalities in its regional economic growth?

There are marked contrasts in prosperity between China's provinces as illustrated on pages 48 and 49. There is a growing gap in living standards between rural and urban China: the agricultural economy is growing at about 3% per annum and the urban economy at more that 20%. The gap is widening each year. This is one of the reasons why some people try to leave China illegally. See extract C, map D and photograph E.

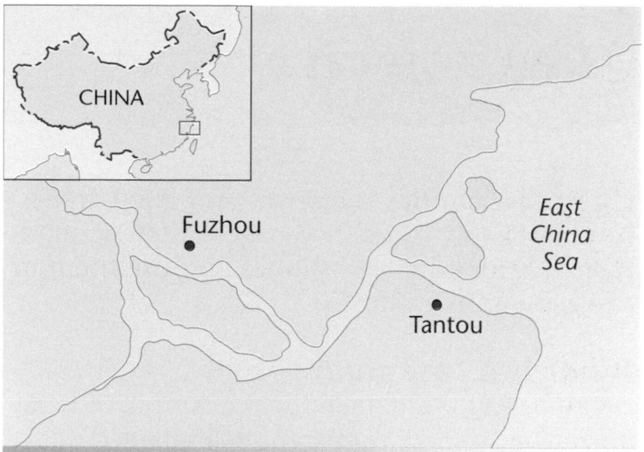

D Location map of Tantou village

A nightmare month-long journey in an overcrowded tugboat followed by 19 days behind bars in Australia and 11 days in a re-education camp back home have done nothing to dampen Xiao Zhang's spirits. "I want to go back to Australia with my whole family. I will try again," the 23-year-old insisted over lunch in his village in Tantou, China. The Tantou area, in Fujian province, is infamous for its illegal immigrants who cross the Pacific Ocean in freighters and rickety fishing boats.

The village of Tantou is a long way from the nice New South Wales beach he and 58 fellow passengers strolled onto last month, changing into suits and seeking a new life. But it is not nearly as poor as many other Chinese villages: illegal immigrants who have fled for Australia, the United States and Europe send back thousands of yuan every month. There is a local saying here: "To find gold, sneak out by boat. One goes, whole family wins gold".

Extract from *South China Morning Post* 23 May 1999

C Risking all for a land of gold

E Tantou village

ACTIVITIES

1 Divide into four groups. Each group is to consider one of the issues summarised on this page and prepare a report for the rest of the class under the following headings:
- explanation of why the issue exists for the Chinese government;
- examples of how the government is attempting to tackle the issue.

Use information from the earlier chapters of this book and from your own research to help you.

2 a) Explain what is meant by the term 'democratic government'.

b) Suggest three reasons why it is difficult for China to have the benefits of a democratic government.

3 Study any recent news items relating to China and give reasons why it might be hindering or supporting China's progress towards being a world superpower.

4 Read again the problems and issues for the Chinese Government (pages 56 and 57 and here). Explain which of these are caused mainly by:
- either, the country's geographical diversity;
- or, its rapid economic growth.

Let's revise

Using **case studies** is essential for good grades in your exam. These two pages are designed to help you identify case studies and use them in the geography exams.

What is a case study?

A case study is a detailed real example of what you have studied, for example a village, factory, farm, region or country. The case studies you have come across in your course (and in this book) have been chosen as typical examples of places or themes in geography. When you use case studies in the exam make sure you use:

- a real example with a name and a location
- an example showing the points you are trying to make.

Revising case studies

How long should they be?

Learn a number of case studies of different scales or size – local, regional and national. There may also be an international or global dimension.

Does it matter where the case studies are in the world?

All geography syllabuses expect you to learn about case studies within the UK plus a range from other parts of the world. A few syllabuses actually name the other countries (check with your teacher whether yours is one of these). Other syllabuses leave the choice to teachers.

When to use a case study

Certain phrases used in exam questions are like clues. They let you know you should use your knowledge about a case study in your answer. Here are some examples of clue phrases:

'Using **an example** from your studies ...'

'**With reference to** an area you have studied ...'

'For a **named** farm/city/region that you have studied ...'

'Use **an example** in your answer ...'

'**Refer to** a study you have made ...'

'**With reference to** your studies ...'

'Choose a city/region/economic activity **you have studied** ...'

'Use a **named example** that you have studied ...'

How to use a case study

When you use a case study:

- do not write down everything you know about it. Pick out the information which fits in with the question being asked;
- make sure that you include facts and figures about your case study as well as using names of places.
- use a labelled sketch map or diagram;
- use geographical terms as much as possible – examples of these can be found in the glossary (pages 63–64) of this book.

Exam questions

Take notice of the **command** words used in the question. Here are some common ones used in questions asking for knowledge about case studies:

- '**describe**' means give facts and figures about a place;
- '**explain**' and '**give reasons**' means to show understanding about what is happening there.

Read the question very carefully before you begin to write your answer. Also you may find it helps to highlight key words (command words, geographical terms, case study clues) and note down some of the basic points needed in your answer, as shown in the example opposite. The example gives i) an exam question, ii) an answer to it which used information on pages 12–13 and iii) comments from an examiner.

Example

i) Question

Read the whole question to avoid overlap and to judge what is needed for each part

a) Using the figures in the table above, calculate China's rate of natural increase of population.

(2 marks)

b) Name the other two factors that must be considered when calculating population change in a country.

(2 marks)

Parts a and b just need brief statements

c) With reference to a named country that you have studied, describe the attempts made to slow down population growth.

(7 marks)

Part c needs a detailed response
Use China 1-child policy, rewards and penalties

ii) Answer

a) China's rate of natural increase of population is 7 per thousand per year.

b) The other factors that must be considered are the number of people coming to live in the country from abroad (immigration) and the number moving out to live elsewhere (emigration).

c) In China the government wanted to lower the population so at first they tried to get couples to marry later and to only have two children. Later they inforced the 1-child policy. Couples need to have permission to have a child and may have to wait a long time for the go-ahead. The government gives special benefits for the first child, such as maternity leave on full pay and they keep the mother's job open for her. Parents in one-child families may get a pay rise, subsidised housing and the child is reserved a free place at school and university.

However, if they have a second child, they have to pay a heavy fine, which is very hard because they are poor. They may lose their job and their house, and their children may not get free places at school. The family also loses the respect of the community and, in some cases, the woman may be forced to have an abortion or be sterilised.

The government says that the policy has been very successful in slowing down the growth of China's population. Other people think that the policy has been ignored in many rural areas by not registering births or by bribing local officials.

iii) Comments

a This is a simple subtraction of the death rate from the birth rate. The units should be included as well for full marks.

b This is accurate, direct and uses the correct terms. No more detail than this is needed to get the full two marks.

c This is a very good answer. The candidate stated in the first sentence which country will be used and she included many facts and figures relevant to the case study. She shows evidence of detailed knowledge and understanding of this topic. Accurate dates, facts and figures, rather than vague, general comments add to the quality of this type of answer. The candidate has still made some sweeping statements, such as "they are poor," which could be more carefully worded. e.g. "most families are poor". The brief evaluation at the end rounds off the answer effectively, although it is essential not to include irrelevant comments.

Spelling, punctuation and grammar (SPG)
This candidate has done very well, with only one spelling mistake. She has used good punctuation and grammar. She will be in the top level for SPG.

Statistics

	UK	CHINA	AUSTRALIA	SOUTH AFRICA	USA
Total area (km^2)	244 880	9 596 960	7 686 850	1 221 040	9 809 431
Total population (millions)	58.3	1 210.0	18.4	44.0	263.6
Population density: people per km^2	243	130	2	35	28

Population

Birth rate (per 1 000) people	13	17	14	27	15
Death rate (per 1 000) people	11	7	7	12	9
Life expectancy (male and female)	74M 79F	69M 72F	77M 83F	54M 58F	73M 79F
Fertility (children per female)	2	2	2	4	2
Population structure: 0–14 15–59 60+	19% 61% 21%	27% 65% 9%	22% 63% 15%	37% 57% 6%	21% 62% 17%
Urban population	90%	29%	86%	57%	77%

Environment and economy

Rate of urban growth per year	0.3%	4.3%	1.4%	3.0%	1.3%
Land use (%): arable grass forest	27 46 10	10 43 14	7% 54% 14%	10 67 4	19 25 30
% workforce in: farming industry services	2 28 70	73 14 13	6% 24% 70%	13 25 62	3 25 72
GNP per person (US$)	$18 700	$620	$18 720	$3 160	$26 980
Unemployment	8.3%	2.8%	8.5%	45%	5.6%
Energy used (tonnes/person/year)	5.40	0.35	7.38	2.49	10.74

Society and quality of life

Infant mortality (deaths per 1000 births)	6	38	5	5.4	7
People per doctor	300	1000	400	1 750	420
Food supply (calories per person per day)	3 317	2 727	3 179	2 695	3 732
Adult literacy	99%	70%	99%	81%	99%
TVs per 1000 people	434	31	666	98	814
Aid received or given per person	$53 given	$3 received	$62 given	$10 received	$33 given
Spending on education (as % of GNP)	5.3	2.4	5.5	3.8	7.0
Spending on military (as % of GNP)	4.0	3.7	2.4	3.0	5.3
United Nations Human Development Index (out of 1.0)	0.92	0.59	0.93	0.71	0.94

Figures are for 1992–97. Source: *Philip's Geographical Digest* (United Nations, World Bank). The Human Development Index is worked out by the UN. It is a summary of national income, life expectancy, adult literacy and education. It is a measure of human progress. In 1992, the HDI ranged from 0.21 to 0.94.

Glossary

accessibility how easy it is to get to a place from other locations 11

acid rain rain with a pH of less than 5.6 that can be harmful to plants and animals 30

adult illiteracy rate the percentage of a country's population unable to read.

alluvium any material that has been deposited by rivers, particularly after flooding 27

arable farming the growing of crops 36

autonomous region areas of China in which minority peoples have partial self-government. These are Inner Mongolia, Ningxia, Xinjiang, Guangxi and Tibet 53

birth rate the number of births in a year for every 1 000 people in a place 12

continental climate a climate which is hot in summer and cold in winter and generally dry. This climate is found inland in large land masses in the mid-latitudes 8

convectional uplift the rising of warmer, lighter air which then cools. This may result in condensation, cloud formation and rainfall 8

crust the thin outer layer of the earth, which includes the continents and the ocean floors 26

death rate the number of deaths in a year for every 1 000 people in a place 12

desertification the changing of an area so that it turns into a desert 29

dykes (or dikes) a mound or embankment built to prevent flooding 25

epicentre the point on the earth's surface directly above the focus of an earthquake 27

ethnic minorities a relatively small number of people within a country, considered by the majority of the population to be different because of their ancestry, culture and customs 58

fault a crack in the rocks, along which movement has taken place 26

floating workers migrant workers who have left their home area to look for work elsewhere, usually in big cities, but do not have a permanent place to live 11

focus the place under the ground where an earthquake starts 26

globalization the increasing spread of common information, ideas and products to all parts of the world 54

godown a factory warehouse, used mainly for storage 18

greenhouse effect the warming of the atmosphere as it absorbs some of the heat given off by the earth. This may be increasing as we put more gases like CO_2 into the air 30

Gross National Product (GNP) a measure of the wealth created by a country's business both at home and abroad 35

growing season the length of time during a year when it is warm enough and wet enough for plants to grow 10

Hong Kong Special Administrative Region on 1 July, 1997, Hong Kong became a special administrative region within China. It will have this status until 30 June 2047 32

human rights the basic rights that any person in the world should be able to claim 58

hydro-electric power energy produced by using the power of running water to turn generators 25,38

incentive an encouragement or reward given for doing something 36,37

infanticide the killing of children with the consent of a parent 14

infant mortality rate the percentage of children dying in childbirth 52

infrastructure the range of communications and other services, such as roads, electricity and water supply, that is needed for economic development to take place 47

international migration the permanent or semi-permanent movement of people from one country to another 12

irrigation artificially adding water to farmland to grow crops 6,29

joint venture company a business partnership involving Chinese and foreign companies 46

Karst scenery the name comes from the Karst region of Slovenia but is now given to any area of limestone which contains, for example, underground streams, caves and dry valleys 41

levée a bank of material along the course of a river. This may be naturally formed by the river depositing alluvium when it floods or by people building artificial banks to prevent flooding 24

life expectancy the age to which a person in a particular place can expect to live 12

load the material being transported in a stream or river 24

loess a fine, silty soil. It can be very fertile, but can also be easily eroded if left unprotected 24,29

magnitude the size or strength of something, such as an earthquake 26,27

manufacturing goods made by hand or with the use of machinery, usually in a factory 46,47

market economy an economy where private individuals or companies can carry out their business with little intervention by the government 37,54

megalopolis a large urban area with more than ten million inhabitants which combines many individual cities 51

migrant a person moving from one country to another, or from one region to another, to settle or to work 16

nullah in Hong Kong, a large drainage channel conveying flood water and sewage into Victoria Harbour 18,19

open city the Treaty of Nanking, 1842, allowed five Chinese cities to become 'open' for trade with Western countries. People from the west were allowed to live in these cities, one of which was Shanghai 20

plateau a large and relatively flat upland area 6

population density the number of people living in a unit of area, e.g. people per square km^2 11

population distribution the way in which people are spread out across an area 10

quotas a limit set on how much should be produced in a given length of time 37

raw materials products obtained from agriculture, forestry, fishing and mining 42

respiratory diseases diseases which affect breathing, such as colds, bronchitis and pneumonia 31

richter scale a scale used to measure the magnitude of earthquakes 27

river basin an area drained by a river and its tributaries 7

river plain an area of flat land crossed by a river 6

satellite town a new town located outside a city, planned as a self-contained community providing work for its inhabitants 20

seismologist a scientist who studies earthquakes 26

soil erosion the removal of soil from an area by any combination of methods such as water, wind or gravity 25,28

special Administrative Region on 1 July 1997, Hong Kong became a special administrative region within China. It will have this status until 30 June 2047 18

state owned enterprises firms owned by the government 56

subsistence wages income received by a person who can provide the bare necessities of life 56

subtropical monsoon climate a climate experienced in areas immediately outside the tropics, in which there is a seasonal change in air flows and rainfall. In winter it is dry; in summer there can be heavy rainfall 50

superpower a large country with a very big population and great military power. Such countries control or influence many other countries 4

terraces steps cut into hillsides to provide flat areas of land for farming and control erosion 25,29

topsoil the surface layer of a soil, which is usually more fertile 28,29

toxic poisonous 31

tributaries smaller streams or rivers flowing into larger ones 25

underemployed a person who has not got enough work to earn a subsistence wage 44

village or ownership enterprise a business not directly agricultural, run within a village or small suburban area, usually operating as part of the market economy 44,45

water table the upper surface of water under the ground. The level to which water fills up a hole dug into the ground 36

weathered broken down by physical, chemical or biological processes 28

World Bank an international banking organisation which obtains money partly from national governments but also from borrowing. It then loans this money to support aid projects in economically developing countries 29

Finding out more about China

Disasters and weather
http://izzy.online.discovery.com

Population
http://www.cpirc.org.cn/eindex.htm

China
http://sun.sino.uni-heidelberg.de/igcs/

Chinese Embassy, Washington
http://www.china-embassy.org/China/China.htm

Chinese Government Internet Information Centre
http://www.chinanews.org/China/indexE.html

CIA Worldfactbook
http://www.odci.gov/cia/publications/factbook/ch.html

The Statistics of China
http://www.umich.edu/~iinet/chinadata/stat/

Maps of China
http://www.chinapage.com/map.html

China Dimensions
http://sedac.ciesin.org/china/

Professional Association for China's Environment
http://www.chinaenvironment.net/

Environmental Protection
http://svr1-pek.unep.net/soechina/index.htm

UN Development Programme data
http://www.undp.org

Unicef data
http://www.unicef.org/sowc98